KAREN BROWN'S

Spanish
Country Inns & Paradors

BOOKS IN KAREN BROWN'S COUNTRY INN SERIES

Austrian Country Inns & Castles

California Country Inns & Itineraries

English, Welsh & Scottish Country Inns

European Country Cuisine - Romantic Inns & Recipes

European Country Inns - Best on a Budget

French Country Bed & Breakfasts

French Country Inns & Chateaux

German Country Inns & Castles

Irish Country Inns

Italian Country Inns & Villas

Portuguese Country Inns & Pousadas

Scandinavian Country Inns & Manors

Spanish Country Inns & Paradors

Swiss Country Inns & Chalets

KAREN BROWN'S

Spanish Country Inns & Paradors

Written by

CYNTHIA & RALPH KITE

Sketches by Barbara Tapp

Cover art by Christina Ladas

Karen Brown's Country Inn Series

WARNER BOOKS

Travel Press editors: Clare Brown, CTC, June Brown, CTC, Karen Brown, Iris Sandilands; technical support: William H. Brown, III

Illustrations: Barbara Tapp
Cover painting: Christina Ladas
Maps: Keith Cassell

This book is written in cooperation with:
Town and Country - Hillsdale Travel
16 East Third Avenue, San Mateo, California 94401

This Warner Books edition is published by arrangement with
Travel Press, San Mateo, California

Travel Press, P.O. Box 70, San Mateo, California 94401, U.S.A.

Warner Books, Inc., 666 Fifth Avenue, New York, NY 10103
 A Warner Communications Company

Printed in the United States of America
Third Printing: April 1989
Fourth Printing: April 1990

Library of Congress Catalog Number: 88-50691

ISBN 0-446-39132-8 (pbk.) (U.S.A.)
        0-446-39131-X (pbk.) (Canada)

TO EACH OTHER

Contents

Introduction

We firmly believe that Spain will cast its spell on you as it did on us. Once we fell under her special enchantment, there was no breaking free, nor any urge to do so - only the desire to return again . . . and again. Even today, Spain is considered somewhat off-the-beaten-track when a trip to Europe is planned, and this is a pity, for Spain has as many, or more, treasures per square kilometer as any other country, plus the added pleasure of being just a bit off-the-beaten-track. Although the country has become "touristized" over the last few decades, there still exist numerous spots where you may find yourselves the only native English speakers in the castle - yes, castle, for private proprietors, as well as the government, have recognized the need for fine hotels in Spain, and have met the demand by creating some of the most charming hotels in all of Europe on or in historical sites. And we have recognized that need by finding and listing accommodations in palaces, old manor homes, traditional inns and monasteries. And many of these are to be found in locations boasting some of the most spectacular sights in Europe.

And, in Spain, there is no need to fret over the possibility of being the only native English speaker in the castle, because nowhere else on the continent will you find people so gracious and willing to communicate and make your stay more enjoyable than here.

Washington Irving, for example, found that to be the case when he visited the fabled Alhambra in Granada in 1829. His "Tales of the Alhambra" evokes the exotic mystery of the palace of the last Moorish king, Boabdil, because Irving stayed there while he wrote. As a modern-day traveler to Granada, you may miss the romance of sleeping in "gloomy apartments" with "bats and owls flitting about" occupied by Irving, but you can check into a convent which is "merely" 500 years old and inside the grounds of the Alhambra itself - filled with antiques, but offering all the modern conveniences - where you'll find yourself a half-day's drive from both the beautiful beaches of the Costa del Sol and year-round skiing in the Sierra

Nevada. And you can discover the rest of Spain - a country with something for everyone: from the birthplace of Don Juan to the birthplace of Hernan Cortés, Conquistador of Mexico; from the tomb of St James the Apostle to the tomb of El Cid, Spain's medieval epic hero. You can visit the plains traversed by Don Quixote in search of wrongs to right and the quixotic architectural achievements of Antonio Gaudí. You can drive the highest road in Europe and visit the largest wildlife refuge. You can see the youthful work of Picasso and the mature work of Salvador Dali. And, to cap it all off, there are beautiful landscapes, fine dining and warm, welcoming people. How can you miss?

PURPOSE OF THIS GUIDE

Our goal has been to discover and describe the most charming and historic hotels in Spain and to design itineraries which will lead you to them by the most scenic and interesting routes. This book should have a special appeal for the traveler looking for a guide to more than the capital city and a handful of highlights; for the visitor who wants to add a little out of the ordinary to his agenda. We do not claim to be objective reporters - that sort of treatment is available anywhere - but subjective, on-site raconteurs. We have definite biases toward those spots we have visited and enjoyed - from tiny hotels in ancient castles to lavish and lovely hotels overlooking the sea. We believe that your choice of accommodation helps to weave the tapestry of your trip. The locations you select to make your bed and break your bread can make or break a visit to any country, and can enhance your memories immeasurably. And, although prices in Spain are playing catch-up with much of the rest of Western Europe, especially in the most popular tourist destinations, there remain many delightful hotel possibilities reasonable enough to allow you the pleasure of indulging yourself. If you follow our itineraries (every one of which we have traveled personally) and trust in our hotel recommendations (every one of which we have visited personally), you will be assured of Spain's best lodging while discovering the country's most intriguing destinations.

BANKS

As a general rule, banks in Spain are open from 9:00AM to 1:30PM, sometimes 2:00, Monday through Friday. Some, most frequently in larger towns, maintain similar business hours on Saturday. Many, but not all, exchange foreign currency: look for a CAMBIO (exchange) sign outside the bank. Often, your hotel or the local tourist office will exchange your dollars, though usually at a slightly less-favorable rate.

CAR RENTAL

This guide is the perfect companion for the traveler who wants to experience Spain by car. We can suggest a couple of international car-rental agencies which we have found to be reasonable and dependable: the Kemwell Group (800 468-0468) and National Car Rental (800 328-4567), though you may have your particular favorite. If you're planning a lengthy trip, you might want to consider leasing or even buying a car in Europe and shipping it home: it's surprisingly uncomplicated if you arrange the purchase in the United States (check with your local foreign-car dealer for details).

CLIMATE

There are three distinct climates in Spain, dividing the country in thirds from north to south.   The northern area is subject to the moderating Atlantic currents and has a relatively good climate for most of the year - too cold to swim in winter, but seldom bitterly cold either; summer is warm, but never extremely hot.   The central plateau is cut off from those moderating currents and has what the Spanish call "nueve meses de invierno y tres de infierno" (nine months of winter and three of hell).   The southern third of the country has a more Mediterranean climate: relatively warm, though damp winters, and often brutal heat in midsummer, which is slightly alleviated along the coastal areas by sea breezes.

CLOTHING

Standards of formality can be generalized: women wear slacks and men need coats and ties almost everywhere they would at home.   In the most elegant city restaurants dresses and coats and ties are common, though only occasionally required.   Skimpy summer attire, though common in resort areas, might still make you feel conspicuous elsewhere.

CREDIT CARDS

Most hotels and many restaurants in Spain accept plastic payment.   All paradors accept all major cards.   In the hotel descriptions we indicate which hotels accept which cards with the following abbreviations: AX = American Express, VS = Visa, MC = Master Card (called Eurocard in Europe), DC = Diner's Club or simply "all major".   You can also get cash with your credit card at most major banks.

CURRENT

You will need a transformer plus an adapter if you plan to take an American-made electrical appliance. Even if the appliance is dual-voltage, as many of them are these days, you'll still need an adapter plug. The voltage is usually 220, but in a few places 110 is used. Occasionally a 110 outlet is provided in the hotel bathroom, but these should be used only for small appliances such as electric razors, since they usually can't handle things like hair dryers. Be sure to check with the manager if the outlet is not clearly marked.

DRIVING

GASOLINE: Gasoline is relatively expensive (perhaps double the U.S. price) and should be considered in your budget if you plan to drive extensively. It is currently a price-regulated item (though deregulation is being discussed), so will cost the same everywhere. Gasoline is available in any small town and at frequent intervals along the freeways. Diesel (called gasoil or gasoleo in Spain) is considerably less costly, but not available at all filling stations. With a little common sense, you should have no trouble finding fuel.

ROADS: Roads in Spain run the gamut from superb freeways to barely-two-lane country roads (and, as you might expect, our countryside itineraries find you more often on the latter). We calculated that, on all but the freeways and a few national highways, we averaged about 50-60 kilometers per hour during our travels. Passing through small towns and sharing the road with trucks make it difficult to beat that average, but the leisurely pace allows you time to enjoy your surroundings as you drive. The personality of the country does not lend itself to an accelerated pace, and neither do the itineraries, because we have taken that into account.

There is order to the Spanish road numbers. A (A6, for example) indicates freeways, N plus a Roman numeral (NIV) indicates major national highways which radiate like spokes from Madrid, N with an Arabic numeral (N403) indicates minor national highways which connect the major ones, C (C321) indicates regional roads, and two letters (which are the first two letters in the name of the province, e.g., TO1234 for Toledo) indicate provincial roads. Their size and the speed possible is usually correspondingly lower as you go down the list from freeways to provincial roads.

Most of the longer freeways are toll roads and every so often require that you pass through a toll booth. When you enter the highway, usually you will be given a ticket with the point of entry marked, and will pay according to mileage accrued when you leave the highway. If you don't know Spanish, look for the amount due on the lighted sign at the booth. While these freeways are excellent and generally uncrowded, the tolls take their toll on your wallet if you drive all day on them. Wherever there are freeways, there are also parallel non-toll highways, but you can expect them to double the driving time between two points.

SEAT BELTS: Almost without exception, use of seat belts is mandatory in Spain, and the law is strongly enforced both in the cities and in the countryside, so get into the habit of buckling up when you get into the car.

TRAFFIC: This is never a problem on the freeways. On smaller roads it can be ferocious. If you're trying to cover a lot of ground in a given day, we suggest that you try to drive during siesta time - between 1:00 and 4:00 - when many trucks and busses stop for lunch. In the large cities, unfamiliarity combined with traffic, parking problems and the fact that almost no two streets are parallel make driving a trial for all but the bravest of souls. Our preference and advice is to leave the car in the hotel parking lot (or one recommended by the hotel) and take cabs or walk around the cities. Underground public parking areas are common and are designated by a rectangular blue sign with a large white "P." In Madrid and Barcelona try the excellent subway systems (called the Metro and marked with signs bearing a large "M"). If you're stopping to visit a town along an itinerary route, we suggest you park on or near a main square (for easy recall), then venture on by foot into those streets that were never designed with cars in mind. It is not uncommon (nor unwise) for parking areas on central streets and plazas to be "vigilados" (overseen) by an attendant, usually wearing something resembling a uniform. He may direct you to a free spot, and will approach you after you park. A tip of 25-50 pesetas is sufficient in this case.

ECONOMY

Though long known as a travel bargain, since its entry into the European Economic Community (EEC), Spain has made appreciable progress toward bringing the cost of its commodities (including tourist facilities) closer to the level of other EEC members. During the reign of Francisco Franco (1939-1975) Spain was generally barred from trade with its democratic neighbors and thus was forced to become self-reliant to the point where it entered the 1980s with the tenth-largest industrial capacity in the world. Currently Spain is aggressively seeking to increase its exports. Tourism accounts for a large share of foreign income, with the number of tourists entering each year exceeding the native population of over 38 million. Fortunately they don't all come at the same time, though the vast majority visits in July and August.

ENGLISH

In the large hotels in the major cities, you won't even need to use your phrase book (we suggest the Berlitz European phrase book, by the way).   And, in the paradors and elsewhere, you'll usually find that someone speaks enough English to ease your way through check-in to check-out.   If not, just pull out your trusty phrase book and point - Spaniards are friendly and you'll eventually make yourself understood (and probably learn some Spanish while you're at it).   If you make advance reservations, be sure to take your letters of confirmation with you: it will save a lot of pointing.

FESTIVALS AND FOLKLORE

By far the five most internationally renowned Spanish festivals are Holy Week (*Semana Santa*, which is celebrated everywhere) and the feria in Seville (the week leading up to Easter and the second week after it, respectively), the festival of San Fermín in Pamplona which features the running of the bulls (the second week of July), the *fallas* in Valencia (the middle of March), the festival of St. James in Santiago (the last two weeks of July) and the carnival in Cadiz (the week in which Ash Wednesday falls).   But every Spanish town has its patron saint, and every saint its day of honor, so there are as many festivals as there are Spanish towns.   If you know where you want to go ahead of time, write the Spanish National Tourist Office or the Oficina de Turismo (Tourist Office) in the town(s) you plan to visit for a list of festival dates so that you might arrange your visit to coincide with one or several of these colorful events.   (Be forewarned, however, that hotel space anywhere will be at a premium and almost always more expensive during festival time.)

FOOD and DRINK

Today, Spanish cuisine is rapidly approaching the international European standard. The government rates restaurants from one to five forks: however, its rating system is based on such matters as the number of choices on the menu and the wine cellar rather than the quality of the food, so it can be misleading. For instance, in order to receive three or more forks, the headwaiter must speak and the menu must be translated into several languages (which often makes for amusing reading) - an achievement which does not reflect upon the dishes served. A modest-appearing and reasonably priced restaurant will often offer good, regional fare.

By far the most common category of food on the Spanish menu is the wide variety of seafood. Many of these are totally unknown to Americans (even where the menu is translated, it doesn't necessarily help). Items such as *angulas* (baby eels), numerous varieties of squid (*calamares*) and octopus (*pulpo*) and similarly numerous shellfish are best viewed as an adventure. You will find many of them excellent and should definitely experiment. Organ meats - such as brains and sweetbreads - are also common and, prepared in many different ways, can be delicious.

If there is any dish more common than seafood, it is the *tortilla española* (spanish omelette) which is made with eggs and potatoes. It will be found on almost every menu as an appetizer or as a main course for the evening meal. It is also often available as a sandwich (*bocadillo*).

There are a few things you should note about the names of eating and drinking establishments. A *BAR* is seldom what we call by that name. It is usually a place where everything from coffee to alcohol is served and is frequented by patrons of all ages. Continental breakfast is served there, too, as are pastries and other desserts. They often also serve simple sandwiches. A *CAFE* is about the same thing, and, indeed, these places are often called *CAFE-BAR* - these are the spots which often have tables outside when the weather permits. A *CAFETERIA* offers a modest, but complete menu and relatively fast service. This seldom involve self service, but provides a less elaborate setting for a meal than the typical restaurant.

Wine is ubiquitous. In the large fancy restaurants a good selection of imported wines is usually available along with the extensive wines of Spain. In smaller ones the list is mostly Spanish, which is often a rich selection indeed, and fun to sample. Probably the best wines come from the Rioja region around Logroño. These are followed by those of the Valdepeñas area of La Mancha, which are slightly more astringent. But there are many other smaller wine-producing regions, some of which we'll point out in the itineraries. If you have no particular favorite, you'll rarely go wrong by requesting the *vino de la casa*, often a wine bottled especially for the restaurant, or else a *vino regional* (regional wine), either *tinto* (red), *blanco* (white) or *rosado* (rose), according to your preference.

Sangría is a national favorite, made from red wine mixed with fresh fruit and liqueur, with infinite variations on that theme, and served over ice. It's a great thirst-quencher and, even if it doesn't appear on the menu, any place will happily drum up a passable *sangría*.

If there is a more common drink than wine in Spain, it is coffee. Spanish coffee is usually served as what we call espresso in the United States. It is thus a small cup of very strong brew to which most people add a considerable amount of sugar. Here are some of the common terms used in ordering: *cafe solo* - a demitasse of espresso; *cafe solo doble* - a double portion of the same; *cafe con leche* - the same coffee with an equal amount of warm milk added to it, often served in a glass and usually taken at breakfast; *cafe cortado* - espresso with just a splash of milk added.

Beer is another favorite, and is always good, sometimes excellent, especially on hot days in a shady plaza. Asking for *una cerveza* will get you a bottle of regional beer or a draught (*cerveza de barril*). *Una caña* will get you a small glass of draught, and the request for *un tanque* will result in a large glass of the refreshing brew.

Another very common beverage ordered in Spanish restaurants is, believe it or not, water: the bottled kind. Though there is nothing wrong with *agua natural* (tap water), *agua mineral* (mineral water) is popular in either *litro* or *medio litro* (liter or half-liter) sizes. It may also be ordered *con* or *sin gas* (with or without carbonation). You'll notice that Spaniards often dilute their wine with it.

Once you leave the large cities and tourist-frequented restaurants, you'll find that menus are poorly translated, or not translated at all. (A good little guide, specializing in menu translation is the "Marling Menu-Master for Spain", by William and Clare Marling.) The following list includes some of the terms of traditional specialties to be found on most Spanish menus:

Desayuno - (breakfast) - This is always a continental breakfast in Spain, consisting of *pan* (bread) and/or *pan dulce* (sweet rolls) along with *café, te* (tea), *leche* (milk) or *chocolate* (hot chocolate). More and more hotels are offering what they call "extras" - *huevos* (eggs), either *revueltos* (scrambled), *fritos* (fried sunny side up), *pasados por agua* (boiled), *poche* (poached), or in a *tortilla* (omelette).

Comida - (lunch) - This is the main meal of the day for most Spaniards and is taken around 2:00PM It normally consists of several courses: *entremeses* (appetizers), *sopas* (soup, usually of the thick variety), *carnes* (meat dishes), *pescados y mariscos* (fish and shellfish), *postres* (desserts) and, of course, *vino*. No one orders all these courses - three or four is most common.

Merienda - (afternoon snack) - This is taken around 6:00PM by many people and may consist of any kind of light food. The most common are *pasteles* (pie or cake, not usually as good as they look in Spain) and *churros* (deep-fried dough, somewhat like a donut but not round, which we would kill for) along with *café* or *chocolate*.

Tapas - (hors d'oeuvres) - This is as much a social tradition as a kind of food and is a feature of after-work bar hopping. Since the variety of tapas is apparently infinite, a good method is to search out a bar where they are on display so you can point. The Spanish government, for health and sanitation reasons, is attempting to force bar owners to stop displaying them except in glass cases, but has not had much success to date. Also available at this time (8:00 to 10:00PM, more or less) are *raciones* (orders, approximately) which are the same things but in larger portions (a *ración* will be a plateful of meatballs, for example, whereas a *tapa* will be just a couple).

Cena - (supper) - This meal has traditionally been taken in Spain after 10:00PM and has been a light meal (one course of the same kinds of things as at lunch). Due to Spain's increasing contact with the rest of Europe in the last decade, customs are changing somewhat. Especially in the larger cities and along the French border, you'll find people eating earlier and restaurants offering a more complete menu at night.

Aceite - (olive oil) - About the only kind of oil used to cook with in Spain and used in many, many dishes.

Carne - (meat) - *Ternera* (technically veal, but really closer to what we call beef) comes in *chuletas* (veal chop, but similar to a T-bone steak if it's thick), *solomillo* (sirloin), *entrecot* (ribeye), *filete* (thinly sliced and pan fried), and *asada* (roasted). *Cerdo* (pork) and *pollo* (chicken) are also commonly found on menus. In central Spain *cochinillo asado* (roast suckling pig) is a common specialty.

Ensalada mixta - (tossed green salad) - Besides lettuce, this usually contains any or all of the following: olive, tomato, onion, tuna, hardboiled egg. But remember that there is only one salad dressing in the entire country: *vinagre* (vinegar) and *aceite* (olive oil).

Gazpacho - Another justifiably famous Spanish dish, it is a cold tomato soup with various spices and olive oil and garnished with bits of bread, bacon, green onions, celery, crumbled egg, etc. You are usually given a choice of garnishes at the table. Gazpacho is one of Spain's Moorish legacies and also has myriad variations even though it is usually called *gazpacho Andaluz* (Andalusian), which is the most popular kind. One common variation in the south is *gazpacho de almendras* (almonds), which is white and has thin sliced almonds floating on top and raisins in it, but tastes pretty much like the regular kind. The soup is an absolutely wonderful cooler if you've been out in the summer heat seeing sights all morning.

Jamon serrano - (cured ham, similar to prosciutto) - A favorite of most Spaniards as a tapa, a bocadillo, or as an added ingredient to another meat dish. There are many varieties and qualities and you'll see them hanging from the ceiling in bars with little cups to catch the juice so it doesn't fall on the customers. *Pata negra* (literally "black foot", a darker variety) is considered the best.

Paella - Probably Spain's best-known dish, it has as many variations as there are Spanish chefs. Based on saffron-flavored rice and olive oil, it may contain any kind of fish, shellfish, chicken, sausage, green peas, beans, bell peppers, or any combination of the above. Because it is complicated to make, it may be offered for a minimum of two people and the menu may warn you that there will be a 20- to 30-minute wait if you order it. Connoisseurs will tell you not to order it in the evening because it will be left over from lunch; but, in our experience, better restaurants make it fresh when you order it.

Pescados y mariscos - (fish and shellfish) - *Rape* (angler fish), *merluza* (hake), *mero* and *lubina* (sea bass), *lenguado* (sole) and *trucha* (trout) are the common fish varieties. *Pez espada* (swordfish, also called *aguja* and *emperador*) is often offered thickly-sliced like steak and can be superb. *Gambas* (shrimp), *langosta* (small variety of lobster), *langostino* (large prawns), *almejas* (clams), and *mejillones* (mussels) are common shellfish. In the northern part of Spain there are also *vieiro* (scallops), *centollo* (spider crab) and *changurro* (sizzling crab casserole). A *zarzuela* is a commonly offered fish stew and has the usual infinite number of variations.

Preparation - Many of the terms describing preparation are relatively meaningless because they simply refer to the origin - *a la Bilbaína*, for example, means Bilbao style, but it never seems to mean the same thing twice. A few terms which are reliable: *al ajillo* (sauteed in garlic), *a la plancha* (grilled), *al pil pil* (sauteed with garlic and olive oil, often with hot pepper), *frito* (fried), *cocido* (stewed), *a la brasa* or *a la parilla* (charcoal broiled), *en brocheta* (skewered), *al horno* (baked in the oven) or *asado* (roasted).

GOVERNMENT

The current government of Spain (since 1975, when Franco died) is a constitutional monarchy similar to Great Britain. The monarchy is hereditary and is balanced by a parliament (called the Cortes). The President is elected in somewhat the same fashion as the British Prime Minister. The traditional regions, such as Catalonia and Andalusia, which grew up during the Middle Ages, have been granted a degree of self control which might be compared to the powers held by the states in the United States. Strong regionalist identification has always been, and still is, characteristic of Spanish politics.

HISTORY

EARLY PERIOD: Traces of cave-dwelling prehistoric man - Neolithic, Megalithic and Magdalenian - have been discovered all over the peninsula. Around the 6th century B.C., the area was widely inhabited by the Celts from the north and the Iberians from Africa. The Phoenicians, the Greeks, and especially the Carthaginians, founded ports at Cadiz (1100 B.C.), Malaga, Huelva and Ampurias (north of Barcelona). As a result of the Second Punic War (second century B.C.), the peninsula became a Roman colony.

ROMAN PERIOD: Hispania was the most heavily colonized of all Rome's dominions and, thus, the basis for modern Spanish culture and its language, legal system and religion all spring from that 600-year period. A number of Roman emperors were born in Spain of either Roman or Hispanic parents, and Julius Caesar himself served there and learned the art of bull fighting. When the entire Roman Empire was overrun by the Germanic tribes from the north, Spain was to suffer the same fate.

VISIGOTH PERIOD: By the 5th century A.D. the Visigoths had subdued the peninsula almost completely (the Basque area was an exception), and had adopted Roman Catholicism as their own. Their feudalistic system saw the origin of the traditional Spanish regions as kingdoms were combined and divided over the next centuries. Their political system involved a monarch who served at the pleasure of the feudal lords and was thus subject to considerable instability as the kaleidoscope of dynastic unions changed constantly. This characteristic strife provided the opportunity, in 711, for the Moors (Islamic Africans) to invade and sweep across the peninsula from south to north in the space of two decades.

MOORISH PERIOD: The Moors were a tolerant people and allowed a diversity of religions to coexist. At that point in history they represented the highest level of civilization in the West and contributed greatly to Spanish culture -

still evident today in Spanish architecture, painting, philosophy and science. Córdoba, by the 10th century, was perhaps the most advanced city in Europe. Nevertheless, the Spanish Christians regrouped in the inaccessible mountains of Asturias to launch a crusade to retake their country from Moslem domination which was to last almost eight centuries.

RECONQUEST PERIOD: Legend has it that a Christian leader named Pelayo set up the Kingdom of Asturias after the first defeat of the Moors at Covadonga in 718. The Christians finally established their capital at León in 914. Under their control were Asturias, Galicia and part of Burgos. They discovered the remains of St James the Apostle in Galicia and he became the patron saint of the Reconquest, as well as an object of devotion for millions of pilgrims who made the difficult journey along the way of St James (through France and across northern Spain) to venerate the holy remains. The pilgrimage to Santiago is still made, albeit by more modern means. By the 11th century, the frontier between the territories of the Christians and the Moors had been fortified with castles as it moved slowly southward and, through various marriages and intrigues, the Kingdom of Castile (the name comes from "castle") had come into existence. During approximately the same period, the Basques began their own process of reconquest which included Catalonia and the eastern coastal areas. During this period border battles were constant both between the Christian kingdoms themselves and between them and the Moors.

By 1248 the Castilian campaign had recaptured most of southern Spain from the Moors, including Seville, conquered by Ferdinand III, later to become St Ferdinand. Castile, now united with Leon, included most of the western half and the south of the peninsula, except for Portugal, which had been established as a separate kingdom in the 11th century.

Meanwhile, the monarchs of Aragón had become supreme on the east side of the peninsula (not to mention in Sicily and Naples) and, when united with Catalonia, ruled from southern France to Valencia. The scene was now set for the transcendental step which would lead to the creation of the modern Spanish nation: the marriage of the heir to the Aragonese throne, Ferdinand V, to the heir to the throne of Castile, Isabella I, thenceforth known as Los Reyes Católicos (The Catholic Monarchs).

MODERN PERIOD: Ferdinand (who was a model prince in Machiavelli's famous work of that name) and Isabella spent most of their reign strengthening the monarchy and expanding their dominions, including financing the expedition of Columbus. Their daughter Juana (the Mad) was too handicapped to rule and so her son Charles was elevated to the throne when Ferdinand died. Charles' father was Phillip the Fair of the Hapsburgs, who were in control of the Holy Roman Empire which included half of Europe and most of the western hemisphere, so Charles also gained the title of Emperor Charles V. His son, Phillip II, to whom he abdicated the crown in 1556, soon added Portugal to his domain. Portugal held an Empire of its own, including Brazil in the New World and Mozambique in Africa, as well as several high-powered trading enclaves in Asia. By the end of the 16th century, Spain's dominions literally ringed the world.

Lions Court
Alhambra

The 17th century saw, however, a serious decline in the monarchy with first Phillip III, then Phillip IV, then Charles II showing a decreasing capacity to rule wisely and an increasing desire to live licentiously on the vast income from their New World mineral riches. During this century Portugal and many of the European territories were lost.

When Charles II died in 1700 without an heir, the Bourbons of France took the throne because Charles' sister had married into that royal family. (The current king, Juan Carlos, is a Bourbon.) The series of Bourbons who ruled during the 18th century - Phillip V, Charles III, Charles IV and Ferdinand VII - proved to be only marginally better than the Hapsburgs who preceded them, so Spain's holdings continued to dwindle, culminating in the loss of all the American possessions (except the Caribbean islands and the Phillipines) by 1825. In 1808, Napoleon seduced the decadent Ferdinand VII with the good life in France, meanwhile installing his own brother on the Spanish throne. The Spaniards reacted swiftly, starting on the *dos de mayo* (the second of May) of the same year, and, with the help of the British (for the first and only time in history), soon regained the crown for Ferdinand. The scene was set for continuing conflict when Ferdinand's brother, Don Carlos, at the head of Basque and Navarrese extremists, disputed Ferdinand's claim to the throne.

The 19th century was thus characterized by three so-called "Carlist Wars" of succession and, in 1898, the Spanish-American War. The Bourbons did manage to hold the throne, but lost the remaining territory of the Empire (Cuba, Puerto Rico, Santo Domingo and the Phillipines). This loss gave rise to widespread intellectual speculation on the causes of Spain's decline by the so-called Generation of 1898.

The early years of the 20th century saw the rise of new populist ideas and continuing labor unrest. In 1923, General Miguel Primo de Rivera established a dictatorship with Alfonso XIII's support. The unrest continued, however, especially in Catalonia and, in 1931, the King was forced to abdicate and go into exile by the Republican, essentially socialist, party which, in the same year, proclaimed the government to be Republican. In 1936 the elections were won by the socialist forces and José Antonio Primo de Rivera, Miguel's son, was head of a rightist revolutionary party. In the same year the revolutionaries began an all-out civil war in the south under the direction of General Francisco Franco. Soon afterward, the Axis powers joined the rebels, whereas the Republicans were supported by the Soviet Union (allegedly in exchange for some 50 metric tons of gold reserves) and the International Brigade. American volunteers served in the Abraham Lincoln Brigade. Ernest Hemingway covered the war as a journalist and later immortalized the brutality of it in "For Whom The Bell Tolls". By 1939, the Franco forces had won the war, over a million Spaniards had died and another half-million were in exile.

As a means of gaining Axis support, Spain had promised to remain neutral in any wars they engaged in and was thus not directly involved in World War II. After the war it found itself somewhat of an outcast in international circles because of its neutrality and generally perceived sympathy to the Axis cause. It finally became a member of the United Nations in 1955 and returned to active diplomatic involvement, but with limited success due to the authoritarian regime headed by "El Caudillo" (the Chief), Generalíssimo Francisco Franco.

In providing for his succession, Franco proclaimed that Spain was a monarchy and Juan Carlos (born in 1938), grandson of Alfonso XIII, would be the future king. When Franco died in 1975, the young king was installed and the process of creating a constitution was begun. The document was approved in 1978 and orderly elections have occurred since that time. The death of Franco did not signify the disappearance of rightist sentiment, however, and, as late as 1981, the right-wing military attempted a coup. Juan Carlos reacted swiftly to put it down and, thus, reassured the world that he was a firmly democratic ruler. Today, Spain is in the throes of transition from an inward-facing, relatively self-dependent nation, to becoming a full partner in the world community.

HOTEL DESCRIPTIONS

This guide is divided into two sections, with hotel descriptions in each. The first section takes you through Spain on researched itineraries, highlights the most interesting sights along the way, and suggests a hotel for each day's destination. The other section is a complete list of hotels ordered alphabetically by town, providing a wide selection of hotels throughout Spain. A detailed description, an illustration and pertinent information is provided on each one. Some are large and posh, offering every amenity and a price to match; others small and cozy (often with correspondingly smaller prices), providing only the important amenities such as private baths, personality and gracious personnel.

For some of you, cost will not be a consideration; for others, it will be a decisive factor. We have been to every hotel which appears in the book, and have tried to include none which don't have a certain charm and personality, no matter what the price. (On occasion, an ideal hotel choice doesn't exist in an itinerary destination, in which case we recommend the best available.) We have indicated what each hotel has to offer and described its setting, so that you can make the choice to suit your own preference, holiday and budget. We feel that if you know what to expect, you won't be disappointed, so we have tried to be candid and honest in our appraisals.

HOTEL RATES AND INFORMATION

The rates hotels charge are regulated by the Spanish government, with inflation causing periodic upward adjustments in prices (usually at the beginning of the year). Most hotels have an intricate system of rates, which vary according to season, local special events, and additional features such as sitting rooms, balconies and views. Prices quoted in this book reflect the 1989 cost in pesetas for a standard double room with private bath for two people during the high season (to which you can expect a six- to twelve-percent tax to be added).   As a general rule, July through October is considered high season in Spain, and, if your schedule allows travel outside these busy months, you can often realize substantial savings.

In Spain, hotels are forbidden by law to make provision of lodging conditional upon patronage of their restaurant.   However, a price is sometimes quoted which includes a continental breakfast, since that is what many people prefer.   Many hotels also have rates for *"pensión completa"* or *"media pensión"* which mean breakfast and either one or two meals, respectively.   These are often an excellent value and should be investigated where convenient.

Children are welcome virtually everywhere in Spain, and you should feel comfortable taking them to any of the hotels in this guide.

HOTEL RESERVATIONS

Whether or not to reserve ahead is not a question with a simple answer; it depends upon the flexibility in your timetable and in your temperament.   It also depends to a large extent on the season in which you are traveling.   For example, during the peak season, accommodation at the Parador Nacional de San Francisco in Granada requires reservations six to eight months in advance.   Other popular hotels with limited rooms are similarly booked, especially those located in spots of particular touristic interest.   Careful travelers make arrangements months in advance to secure desirable accommodations during a local festival.   On the other hand, throughout much of the year space can be obtained in most places with a day's notice, or less.   For those who prefer security (and who are going in the summer months) there are several ways of making reservations:

TRAVEL AGENT: A travel agent can be of great assistance in handling all of the details of your holiday and "tying" it all together for you in a neat little package including hotel reservations, airline tickets, boat tickets, train reservations, etc. For your airline tickets there will be no service fee, but most travel agencies make a charge for their other services. The best advice is to talk with your local agent. Be frank about how much you want to spend and ask exactly what he can do for you and what the charges will be. Although the travel agency in your town might not be familiar with all the little places in this guide, since many are so tiny that they appear in no other major sources, lend them your book - it is written as a guide for travel agents as well as for individual travelers.

LETTER: If you start early, you can write to the hotels directly for your reservations. Be brief in your request. When you receive a reply, send the deposit requested (if any) and ask for confirmation of receipt. Note: when corresponding with Spain be sure to spell out the month since, in Europe, they reverse our system - 7/8 means the 7th of August, not the 8th of July. Since the mail to Spain tends to be slow, especially outside the large cities, you should allow 6 weeks for a reply. Although most hotels can find someone able to understand a letter in English, we have provided a reservation-request letter written in Spanish with an English translation. Following this format you can tailor a letter in Spanish to meet your requirements. The translation includes phrases which will enable you to request specific features, such as sea view, balcony and suite. Check the hotel's description for recommendations in this regard before writing.

SAMPLE RESERVATION REQUEST LETTER

HOTEL NAME & ADDRESS - clearly printed or typed

Muy señores nuestros:

Rogamos reserven para _____ *noche(s)*
We are writing to request a reservation for   (number of)   night(s)

a partir del día ____ *de* _____ *hasta el día* ____ *de* _____
From   (date) of (month)   to   (date) of   (month).

(Months are *enero* (January), *febrero, marzo, abril, mayo, junio, julio, agosto, septiembre, octubre, noviembre, diciembre*)

_____ *habitacion(es) sencilla(s)*   *con cama extra* - with an extra bed
single room(s)   *con vista al mar* - with a sea view
   con terraza - with a terrace

_____ *habitacion(es) doble(s)*   *con vista a la plaza* - facing the plaza
double room(s)   *con vista al patio* - facing the patio
   en piso alto - on an upper floor

_____ *habitacion(es) con salón*   *en piso bajo* - on a lower floor
room(s) with sitting room   *en la parte antigua* - in the old part

Somos _____ *personas.*
We have (number of) persons in our party.

Les rogamos avisen de la disponibilidad de la(s) habitacion(es), el precio de la(s) misma(s), y el depósito requerido. En espera de su respuesta les saludamos, atentamente,
Please advise availability, the rate and the deposit necessary. Awaiting your reply, we remain, sincerely,

YOUR NAME & ADDRESS - clearly printed or typed

TELEPHONE: Another method of making reservations is to call. The cost is minimal if you dial direct on a weekend (business days for hotels), and the advantage great since you can have your answer immediately (though you should still request written confirmation). If space is not available, you can look right away for an alternative. Remember that Spain is six hours ahead of New York for most of the year and time your call accordingly. Basically, the system is to dial the international access code (011), followed by the country code for Spain (34), then the city code (noted in parentheses) and local telephone number listed in the hotel descriptions. (If calling from within Spain, you will need to dial just 9 instead of 01134.)

TELEX/TELEFAX: If you have access to a telex or facsimile machine, this is another efficient way to reach a hotel. When a hotel has a telex or fax available we have included the number(s) in the description section. Again, be sure to specify your arrival and departure dates and what type of room(s) you want. And, of course, include your telex or fax number for their response. When using a fax, remember that you must include the city code noted in parentheses before the telephone numbers in the hotel descriptions.

U.S. REPRESENTATIVE: A few of the hotels we've recommended and all of the paradors have a U.S. representative through which reservations can be made. If time is short, this can prove a convenient and efficient method of reserving accommodation, particularly if you can make multiple reservations with one phone call. The service is not free, sometimes charging as much as 25% over the normal room rate, and payment in advance is required. Be as specific about your room preferences with the representative as you would be with the hotel, so that you will get exactly what you want. (Reservations [free of charge] can also be made through the paradors' central reservation office in Madrid. See page 28.)

In addition to the representatives listed in the hotel descriptions, with this printing, we would like to introduce Eugenio Ovalle, a very capable man with extensive knowledge of Spain. Reservations can be made at hotels and paradors through his company, ALTATOURS. (AltaTours, 870 Market Street, Suite 784, San Francisco, Ca., 94102, Tel: (415) 777-1307, (800) 338-4191, Fax: (415) 434-2684)

INFORMATION

A rich source for free information about Spain is the Tourist Office of Spain: Princesa 1, Torre de Madrid, 28008 Madrid, (1) 241-2325; or 665 Fifth Ave., New York, NY 10022, (212)759-8822; or Water Tower Place, Suite 915 East, 845 North Michigan Ave., Chicago, IL 60611, (312)642-1992; or 8383 Wilshire Blvd., Suite 960, Beverly Hills, CA 90211, (213)658-7193. They can provide you with general information about the country or, at your request, specific information about towns, regions and festivals. Local tourist offices (*oficina de turismo*) are found in most small towns throughout the country, with those in the regional capitals providing colorful and informative brochures on the surrounding area. They are usually easy to find usually and should be a ritual stop for the sightseer, offering an incomparable on-site resource, furnishing town maps and details on local and regional highlights.

ITINERARIES

The first section of this guide features itineraries covering most of Spain. They may be taken in whole or in part, or tied together for a longer journey. Each of the itineraries highlights a different region of the country, and they are of different lengths, enabling you to find one or more to suit your individual tastes and schedule. They are designed to accommodate customization.

We have intentionally not specified how many nights to stay at each destination. Your personality and time restraints will dictate what is best for you. Some travelers wish to squeeze as much as possible into their allotted vacation time, even if it means rising with the sun and never settling more than one night in any destination. Others, ourselves included, prefer to concentrate their time in fewer locations in order to relax, unpack and savor the atmosphere and novelty of the spot. If you're new to Spain and planning a trip there, we hope that, upon reading through the itineraries and hotel descriptions, you'll get a feel for which places merit the most time and which can be done justice with an overnight stay. In other words, this guide should be a reference and not a prescription for your personalized trip.

Keep in mind that the hotels recommended in the itineraries represent only about half of those described in this guide. There are alternate choices in the hotel listing, which are also indicated by stars on the itinerary maps, so, if your first choice is booked, or you're wandering off the itineraries, other recommended hotels are to be found throughout the country.

MAPS

Accompanying each itinerary is a map showing the routing and places of interest along the way. These are artist's renderings and are not meant to replace a good commercial map. Before departure, you should procure a detailed map with highway numbers, expressways, alternate routes and kilometrage. There is a Michelin red series (1:1,000,000) map of all of Spain and seven regional (yellow series, 1:400,000) maps. These are exceptionally good resources and they tie in with the Michelin "Green Guide" for Spain which is an excellent source for more detail on sights, museums and places of interest.

Between the itinerary section and the hotel listing, you'll find a map showing the locations of the towns in which we have recommended hotels. Each is marked with a number, which will help you locate the nearest recommended hotel to your chosen destination (or nearby alternates should your first choice be unavailable). These map numbers are cross-referenced in the hotel listing and indices.

PARADORS

The Spanish government operates a system of hotels called *paradors* (literally "stopping places") which are widely acknowledged to constitute the most outstanding bargain in the country for quality received. While you could travel throughout Spain staying practically nowhere but in paradors we also recommend a variety of other charming hotels. In the hotel section, beginning on page 176, we have given in-depth descriptions of our favorite paradors along with many other wonderful choices of places to stay. The abbreviation P.N. (for Parador Nacional) before the hotel name indicates which are paradors.

The first paradors were created in 1928 in a effort to encourage tourists to those areas lacking adequate hotel facilities. New ones have been added periodically ever since. (Watch for upcoming additions in Ronda, Cuenca and Santiponce.) Many are imaginatively installed in remodeled historic buildings, while others are modern constructions built in creative regional style. While each is unique, the standard of service and quality of accommodation are consistently high. Another bonus is that there are almost always signs which lead you from the edge of the town to the parador by the most efficient route. This may seem a minor advantage, but it can save time and frustration.

All paradors have good to excellent dining rooms serving regional culinary specialties from a set menu or a la carte. They do not specialize in light fare, however, so be prepared to eat substantially, and to pay between 2,000-2,500 pesetas per person. If you follow the Spanish tradition of taking your big meal at midday, paradors provide good stopping places en route.

To maintain their standards the paradors are periodically closed for remodeling. You can check on closures and receive information about the government chain by writing to: Paradores de Turismo, Velázquez 18, 28001 Madrid, or the Tourist Office of Spain. The parador system also has a central reservation office (*central de reservas*) through which you can make reservations at any hotel in the network free of charge.   They speak English, can advise you of availability immediately, and will follow up with written confirmation.   Usually a deposit is not required unless a stay of more than two nights is planned in one parador.   Again, the most efficient way to use this service is to make all of your parador reservations with a single phone call, if possible.   Their hours are 9:30-1:30 and 4:30-7:30 Monday through Friday.   Phone: (1) 435-9700, -44 and -68; telex: 44607; fax: 435-9944.

Below is a complete list of paradors:

AIGUABLAVA, P.N. Costa Brava, beach, modern, (72)622162, 11,000
ALARCON, P.N. Marqués de Villena, city, castle, (66)331350, 10,000
ALBACETE, P.N. La Mancha, outskirts, regional style, (67)229450, 6,500
ALCAÑIZ, P.N. La Concordia, city, castle, (74)830400, 9,000
ALMAGRO, P.N. de Almagro, city, convent, (26)860100, 8,500
ANTEQUERA, P.N. de Antequera, city, regional style, (52)840261, 8,000
ARCOS DE LA FRONTERA, P.N. Casa del Corregidor, city, regional style, (56)700500, 9,500
ARGOMANIZ, P.N.P. de Argómaniz, highway, palace, (45)282200, 7,000
ARTIES, P.N. D. Gaspar de Portolá, mountains, modern, (73)640801, 8,000
AVILA, P.N. Raimundo de Borgoña, city, palace, (18)211340, 8,500
AYAMONTE, P.N. Costa de la Luz, outskirts, modern, (55)320700, 8,000
BAILEN, P.N. de Bailén, highway, modern, (53)670100, 6,500
BAYONA, P.N. Conde de Gondomar, beach, historic property, (86)355000, 11,000
BENAVENTE, P.N. Rey Fernando II de León, city, castle, (88)630300, 8,000
BENICARLO, P.N. Costa del Azahar, beach, modern, (64)470100, 8,500
BIELSA, P.N. Monte Perdido, mountains, modern, (74)501011, 8,500
CADIZ, Hotel Atlántico, city, modern, (56)226905, 10,000
CALAHORRA, P.N. Marco Fabio Quintiliano, city, modern, (41)130358, 8,000
CAMBADOS, P.N. El Albariño, city, regional style, (86)542250, 8,500
CAÑADAS DEL TEIDE, P.N. de Las Cañadas del Teide, mountains, modern, (22)332304, 6,000
CARDONA, P.N. Duques de Cardona, city, castle, (3)8691275, 7,000
CARMONA, P.N. Alcázar del Rey D. Pedro, city, historic property, (54)141010, 10,500
CAZORLA, P.N. El Adelantado, mountains, modern, (53)721075, 8,500
CERVERA DE PISUERGA, P.N. Fuentes Carrionas, mountains, modern, (88)870075, 8,000

CEUTA, Hotel La Muralla, city, historic property, (56)514940, 10,000
CHINCHON, P.N. de Chinchón, city, convent, (1)8940836, 10,000
CIUDAD RODRIGO, P.N. Enrique II, city, castle, (23)460150, 9,000
CORDOBA, P.N. La Arruzafa, city, modern, (57)275900, 10,500
FERROL, P.N. de Ferrol, city, regional style, (81)356720, 7,500
FUENTE DE, P.N. Rio Deva, mountains, modern, (42)730001, 7,500
FUENTERRABIA, P.N. El Emperador, city, castle, (43)642140, 9,500
FUERTEVENTURA, P.N. de Fuerteventura, beach, modern, (28)851150, 8,000
GIJON, P.N. Molino Viejo, city, modern, (85) 370511, 9,000
GRANADA, P.N. San Francisco, city, convent, (58)221440, 14,500
GREDOS, P.N. Isla de Gredos, mountains, modern, (18)348048, 8,000
GUADALUPE, P.N. Zurbarán, city, convent, (27)367075, 8,000
HIERRO, EL, P.N. Isla de El Hierro, beach, regional style, (22)558036, 8,000
JAEN, P.N. Castillo de Santa Catalina, outskirts, historic property, (53)264411, 9,000
JARANDILLA DE LA VERA, P.N. Carlos V, city, castle, (27)560117, 8,500
JAVEA, P.N. Costa Blanca, beach, modern, (65)790200, 10,500
LEON, Hotel San Marcos, city, historic building, (87)237300, 11,500
MALAGA, P.N. Gibralfaro, city, modern, (52)221903, 9,000
MANZANARES, P.N. de Manzanares, highway, modern, (26)610400, 6,000
MAZAGON, P.N. Cristóbal Colón, beach, modern, (55)376000, 10,000
MELILLA, P.N. D. Pedro del Estopiñán, city, modern, (52)684940, 8,000
MERIDA, P.N. Via de la Plata, city, convent, (24)313800, 9,500
MOJACAR, P.N. Reyes Católicos, beach, modern, (51)478250, 9,000
NERJA, P.N. de Nerja, beach, modern, (52)520050, 11,000
OLITE, P.N. Principe de Viana, city, castle, (48)740000, 9,000
OROPESA, P.N. Virrey Toledo, city, castle, (25)430000, 8,000
PONTEVEDRA, P.N. Casa del Barón, city, palace, (86)855800, 8,500
PUEBLA DE SANABRIA, P.N. de Puebla de Sanabria, highway, modern, (88)620001, 7,500
PUERTO-LUMBRERAS, P.N. de Puerto-Lumbreras, highway, modern, (68)402025, 6,500
RIBADEO, P.N. de Ribadeo, city, modern, (82)110825, 8,500
SALAMANCA, P.N. de Salamanca, city, modern, (23)268700, 9,000
SALER, EL, P.N. Luis Vives, beach, modern, (6)1611186, 11,000
SAN SEBASTIAN DE LA GOMERA, P.N. Conde de la Gomera, city, modern, (22)871100, 11,000
SANTA CRUZ DE LA PALMA, P.N. de Sta. Cruz de la Palma, city, modern, (22)412340, 7,000

SANTIAGO DE COMPOSTELA, Hotel Reyes Católicos, city, historic building, (81)582200, 16,000
SANTILLANA DEL MAR, P.N. Gil Blas, city, palace, (42)818000, 11,000
SANTO DOMINGO DE LA CALZADA, P.N. de Santo Domingo de la Calzada, city, palace, (41)340300, 8,500
SEGOVIA, P.N. de Segovia, outskirts, modern, (11)430462, 10,000
SEO DE URGEL, P.N. de Seo de Urgel, city, modern, (73)352000, 6,500
SIERRA NEVADA, P.N. de Sierra Nevada, mountains, modern, (58)480200, 7,500
SIGÜENZA, P.N. Castillo de Sigüenza, city, castle, (11)390100, 8,500
SORIA, P.N. Antonio Machado, city, modern, (75)213445, 8,500
SOS DEL REY CATOLICO, P.N. Fernando de Aragón, city, regional style, (48)888011, 7,000
TERUEL, P.N. de Teruel, city, modern, (74)602553, 8,500
TOLEDO, P.N Conde de Orgaz, outskirts, modern, (25)221850, 11,000
TORDESILLAS, P.N. de Tordesillas, highway, modern, (83)770051, 8,000
TORREMOLINOS, P.N. Del Golf, beach, modern, (52)381255, 11,000
TORTOSA, P.N. Castillo de la Zuda, city, castle, (77)444450, 8,000
TRUJILLO, P.N. de Trujillo, city, convent, (27)321350, 8,500
TUY, P.N. San Telmo, city, regional style, (86)600309, 8,500
UBEDA, P.N. Condestable Davalos, city, palace, (53)750345, 10,000
VERIN, P.N. Monterrey, outskirts, modern, (88)410075, 7,500
VICH, P.N. de Vich, mountains, modern, (3)8887211, 9,000
VIELLA, P.N. Valle de Arán, mountains, modern, (73)640100, 8,000
VILLAFRANCA DEL BIERZO, P.N. de Villafranca del Bierzo, highway, modern, (87)540175, 6,500
VILLALBA, P.N. Condes de Villalba, city, castle, (82)510011, 10,000
ZAFRA, P.N. Hernán Cortés, city, castle, (24)550200, 8,000
ZAMORA, P.N. Condes de Alba y Aliste, city, palace, (88)514497, 9,000

PLAZAS

It may be helpful to understand the general layout of most of the cities and towns of Spain. The central point of most is the main plaza, often referred to as the *plaza mayor*. Some larger cities like Madrid have a central plaza in the old quarter plus others in the more recently constructed parts of town. Small cities have just one main plaza in the center of the old quarter and in the vicinity you most want to visit.

The main plaza is frequently the most lively area of the city and it is often surrounded by shops and outdoor cafes. This will typically be the area where the ancient custom of the *paseo* or evening stroll takes place. The cathedral is also usually here as are other historic buildings. They serve as excellent orientation points.

SECURITY WHILE TRAVELING

Most Spaniards are friendly, gregarious and gracious. They are helpful and open to tourists. You will generally feel welcome in their country. As in any other country, however, there are a few people who see tourists as targets for crime. The problems are basically purse-snatching and breaking into cars and are by and large limited to the larger cities. The answer is caution and common sense. Especially in crowded areas, be cautious with your wallet or purse. Don't leave anything in your car, ever. Lock your valuables in the hotel safe. Carry traveler's checks rather than large amounts of cash. In other words, take the same precautions you would at home.

SIESTA

Except for restaurants, almost every place of business closes for two to three hours sometime between 1:00 and 5:00. This includes all but the largest tourist attractions (e.g. The Prado), most stores (El Corte Inglés and Galerías Preciados department stores are exceptions) and offices. (Banks don't reopen to the public in the afternoon.) So, about the only activities in which to engage during the siesta are dining, drowsing or driving. You will most likely find "Spanish time" easy to adapt to.

TELEPHONES

It is quite a bit more expensive to call the United States from Spain than vice versa but, should you want to, the most economical method is to search out the local *telefonica* (telephone office), where you simply give the operator the phone number, after which she will place the call, indicate the booth for you to take it in once it's placed, and tell you how much it cost afterward. Few hotels feature direct-dial capability to the United States (though it is becoming more common to find it available for domestic and European calls), so a call home will most likely be placed for you by the hotel receptionist, for a surcharge that varies between reasonable and shocking. To avoid an unpleasant surprise, inquire how long-distance calls are charged before placing one.

TIME

A very important aspect of traveling in Spain is to acclimate yourself to the national time schedule. Breakfast is at the same time as at home. The main meal, however, is almost exclusively eaten at around 2:00PM. Most restaurants open around 1:00 and close about 4:00. It is during these hours that they offer their main menu and can be expected to have almost everything on it. They open again at about 8:30 or 9:00 for dinner, which is normally a light meal and is eaten up to 10:00 or 11:00, and, in some spots, even 12:00. Traditionally, restaurants have a reduced menu in the evening, although it seems that nowadays more and more establishments are offering the same fare at night as at midday, as Spain becomes increasingly "Europeanized", a process which is taking place rapidly and, logically enough, from north to south in the country. In Catalonia and the Basque country, you'll find that restaurants close earlier - a fact that even astounds many Spaniards we've talked with. Restaurants that cater to tourists - such as the parador dining rooms - are the most flexible in this regard, and will normally offer a full menu in the evening. We feel it is most comfortable to adjust to the Spanish schedule if possible. You may find the service less than perfect if you take a table at a busy restaurant at 2:00 and order only a sandwich, and you may be disappointed if you expect to have a five-course dinner in the evening. Between the *tapas* (munchies) available at all bars at almost all times, and the numerous *cafeterias* where small, quick meals can be had at any hour, you won't starve.

TIPPING

As everywhere, tipping is not a simple matter on which to give advice. Most restaurants and hotels include "*servicio*" in the bill but a small tip will not come as a surprise when the service is good, especially in restaurants frequented by tourists. Small means different things to different people but certainly should not exceed 5%. In informal bars and cafeterias no tip is expected.

TRAINS

The Spanish National Railways (called RENFE) has an extensive network of trains throughout the country. There are express trains (called the Talgo) between Madrid and the larger cities, and somewhat slower ones to almost everywhere else. They often offer several discount schemes which can be very good values - the Eurailpass is a bargain for those who are traveling extensively in Europe. The Spanish National Railway is represented in the U.S. by the French National Railroads, 610 Fifth Ave., New York, 10020, (212)582-2110, or you can call San Francisco on (415)582-2110.

On weekends, from May to October, RENFE offers day tours from Madrid. (Their departure schedules vary, so be sure to verify dates.) They offer a superior, trouble- and traffic-free travel bargain. These day excursions include transportation and guided tours (with free time for lunch), and cost 1,450 to 1,950 pesetas per person (1,000 for children under 12). Their destinations are Aranjuez, Toledo, Avila, Siguenza and Alhama de Aragon (with a visit to the Monasterio de Piedra). With the exception of the Aranjuez trip, which departs from the Delicias station on the reconstructed, steam-driven *Tren de la Fresa* (Strawberry Train), the day trips originate from the Chamartin train station. Tickets can be purchased at the station or RENFE ticketing offices in Madrid.

Introduction

RENFE also offers two-day excursions from Madrid leaving early Saturday morning and returning late Sunday evening. They include transportation, guided tours, en route visits, overnight lodging, folkloric events and wine-tasting (free time is alloted for meals). The prices vary according to class of train and hotel accommodation. The following is a list of excursions available in 1989 and their lowest and highest per-person rates based on two people sharing a hotel room:

Tren Ciudad Monumental de Caceres: Pts 9,745 - 12,640.
Tren Tierras del Cid: Pts 12,775 - 15,225.
Tren Ciudad Encantada de Cuenca: Pts 10,300 - 13,315.
Tren Valladolid: Cuna del Descubrimiento: Pts 7,150 - 10,865.
Plaza Mayor de Salamanca: Pts 9,850 - 13,825.
Camino de Soria: Pts 6,950 - 8,925.
Tren Romanico de Zamora: Pts 6,450 - 9,050.
Tren Camino de Santiago Palentino: Pts 6,975 - 7,750.

Tickets can be purchased in Madrid at Terminal de Juliatours, Gran Via, 68, tel: 2489605; Terminal de Trapsatur, San Bernardo, 23, tel: 2416321; and Terminal de Pullmantur, Plaza de Oriente, 8, tel: 2411805.

RENFE has an answer to the famous Orient Express: the *Al-Andalus Expreso*. In May, June, September and October, the luxurious *belle-epoque* train travels weekly between Seville and Malaga, visiting Granada and Cordoba en route. In July and August, it journeys between Pamplona and Santiago de Compostela, with interim stops in Leon and Burgos. The elegant trips last two very full days and a night and include private cabins and on-board meals. Available through travel agents at home and in Spain, the excursion costs 60,000 pesetas ($530.00 US) per person, double occupancy (1989 rate). For more information write to RENFE, or call 1-800-992-3976 in the United States (203-454-8916 in Connecticut).

Madrid Highlights

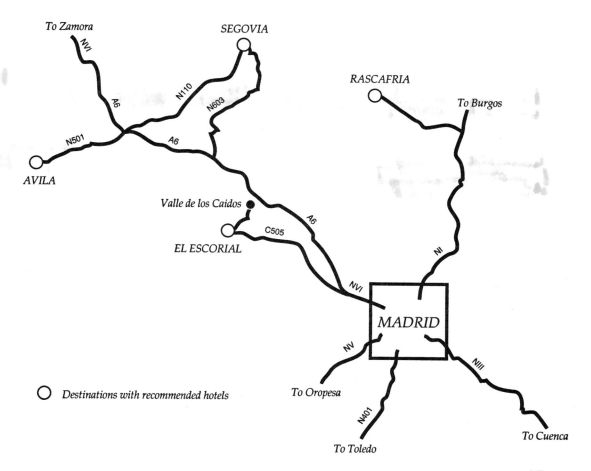

To Zamora
NVI
SEGOVIA
RASCAFRIA
To Burgos
N110
N603
A6
N501
A6
AVILA
Valle de los Caidos
A6
NI
C505
EL ESCORIAL
NVI
MADRID
NV
NIII
To Oropesa
To Cuenca
N401
○ Destinations with recommended hotels
To Toledo

Madrid Highlights

We rediscover Madrid with increasing pleasure each time we are there, mingled with increasing astonishment at the "new" face of the city which has emerged since Franco's death in 1975. It is a big, vigorous city - comparable in size to other western European capitals - but a comfortable one for the first-time visitor. Madrid's attractions will not overwhelm you if you have only a few days to devote to the city, but offer more than enough diversity and stimulation for a longer stay. If you are experiencing Madrid for the first time, a popular method of familiarization is to take one of the numerous city tours available in English (ask at the front desk of your hotel). You will get an idea of the city layout, and can return at your convenience to spend more time in places that pique your interest, or you may prefer to strike out on your own from the start, armed with a detailed sightseeing guide, a good city map (available at any bookstore or newsstand kiosk) and your sense of adventure.

Plaza Mayor
Segovia

A car is more trouble than it is worth in Madrid, which shares the traffic problems common to all large cities. If your visit here is at the outset of your trip, we suggest that you not get your car until you are ready to leave and, if Madrid is your last stop, that you turn your car in the day you get here. Otherwise, leave your car in a protected parking lot for the duration of your stay.

The major things to do and see are often within walking distance of downtown hotels, or readily accessible by "metro", the easily understood and extensive subway system that transports you swiftly and inexpensively to every important intersection in the city. Cabs are also reasonable for trips around town. But walk when you can, because downtown Madrid is made for wandering - with wide bustling boulevards lined with gracious old-world buildings and lively outdoor cafes, and narrow old streets winding through colorful neighborhoods and picturesque plazas. Below we mention a few of our favorite sights.

Probably the greatest attraction in the city is the Prado Museum. Its facilities are gradually being expanded and upgraded, and it boasts one of the finest permanent art collections in Europe, as well as popular and well-presented special exhibitions. Most of the private collections of the Spanish monarchs are here. As with the Louvre in Paris or the Ufizzi in Florence, you could spend days here and still not do justice to its treasures. Depending on your knowledge of and interest in the arts, we suggest you either take a tour of the museum's highlights (private if possible), or purchase a guidebook, study the directory and set out in search of your particular favorites. The best of Goya, Velazquez, El Greco and Murillo are here and should be seen, if nothing else. Picasso's famous "Guernica" is housed in a special annex, and splendidly displayed along with numerous sketches leading up to the final product. To reach the Casón del Buen Retiro (where it was placed after it was returned by the New York's Metropolitan Museum a few years ago), walk east on the street on the north side of the Prado, and you will see it on your left just as you reach the park. There are some fine art galleries along the way.

The Parque del Buen Retiro across the street is an enormous Central Park-like haven where *madrileños* stroll, bike, boat and relax at all hours. The park also hosts outdoor concerts and theater (check the local paper or ask at your hotel desk for information).

A short distance south of the Retiro Park, near the Atocha train station on Calle Fuenterrabía, is the fascinating Royal Tapestry Factory (Real Fábrica de Tapices) where tapestries are being made as they have been since the 18th century, as well as some original tapestry drawings by Goya.

The neo-classic Royal Palace, at the west end of downtown, was conceived by Phillip V, but first occupied by Charles III. Napoleon proclaimed it the equal of Versailles, and it is definitely worth a visit. The extensive grounds and rooms, each a veritable art museum, will provide a glimpse of how the Bourbons lived during their heyday in Spain. The beautiful Plaza de Oriente (so named because it lies on the east side of the palace) is downtown's largest and is adorned with over forty statues of Spanish and Visigothic royalty, with an equestrian statue of Phillip IV at its center.

If you are traveling with children, you would probably enjoy a visit to the huge Casa de Campo where there is a nice zoo (with one of the first pandas born in captivity), an amusement park and a lake. The area used to be the royal hunting grounds.

Just southeast of the Royal Palace is the heart of the old city and one of the most monumental squares in the country, the 17th century Plaza Mayor. An excellent place to people-watch from an outdoor cafe, the old plaza is completely enclosed by tall historic buildings, and has a statue of Phillip III in the middle. If you exit the plaza through the Arco de los Cuchilleros (on the south side) you will discover many typical bars and restaurants, Casa Paco and the atmospheric Casa Botín (known for its roast suckling pig), on streets which take you back in time. The Posada de la Villa, on nearby Cava Baja street, is another colorful spot for a mid-day meal.

There is a colorful flea market, called El Rastro, a few blocks south of the Plaza Mayor on Ribera de Curtidores street. Though it operates every day, Sunday is the liveliest time to go. Absolutely everything is sold here, both in permanent shops and temporary booths, and madrileños and tourists alike shop here in droves. You may even find some genuine antiques at bargain prices, but "buyer beware" is the rule here. Haggling over prices (*regateando*) is also appropriate at El Rastro, unlike most other places in Spain.

About halfway between the Royal Palace and the Prado Museum is the huge plaza called Puerta del Sol. This is the center of activity in downtown Madrid and, in a sense, the center of Spain because all of the main highways (those designated with an "N") radiate from here. Inlaid into the sidewalk on one side of the plaza you will find a plaque marking "*Kilometro 0*". Some of the city's best shopping is to be found in the immediate vicinity, including a bustling pedestrian street lined with boutiques. To the northwest on Calle Preciados is the main store of Corte Inglés and, at the end of that street on Plaza Callao, is Galerías Preciados (both large department stores which you will see in all the larger cities of Spain). The Corte Inglés has a slightly classier line of goods at slightly higher prices. It is also useful to remember that these stores, unlike most smaller shops, stay open through the siesta period.

Shopping for antiques can be fun in Madrid. The largest concentration of antique shops is in the area southeast of the Puerta del Sol, especially on Calle del Prado between the Plaza de Santa Ana and the Plaza de las Cortes.

For archaeology buffs, Madrid has two excellent museums. The Museo Arqueológico, which is at the north end of the Paseo de Recoletos near the Columbus (Colón) monument, emphasizes Iberian and classical material and includes the famous Dama de Elche. On the northwest side of town, near the university, is the Museo de America (temporarily closed for remodeling), which has an outstanding collection of pre-Colombian material from the New World.

The Centro de Arte Reina Sofia should also be investigated. It has developed a fine reputation for the quality of its rotating exhibits.

Madrid's night scene has something for everyone - from elegant dining and highbrow cultural events to colorful hole-in-the-wall tapa bars and pulsating new-wave discotheques. Progressive and relatively liberal administrations following Franco's death have opened the door to new freedoms (or license, depending on your point of view) not experienced here as little as 15 years ago. The lifting of Franco's severe censorship has paved the way not only for pornography, fast food, rock music and divorce, but also for political argument, public gatherings and displays of affection without fear of retribution; and you will most likely witness all of the above. Spain's recently condoned freedom of expression is nowhere as colorful and varied as in her capital city. Today, those same silent streets that were monitored by civil guards under Franco are not rolled up until dawn in many areas throughout Madrid. One of the liveliest (and safest) late-night spots in the city is located about halfway between the Cibeles fountain and the Columbus monument on the Paseo de Recoletos. Here indoor and outdoor cafes, like the Cafe Gijón, hum with the nation's favorite pastime: conversation.

There are new restaurants which evoke the best of Paris and New York (and, indeed, are modeled carefully after them), including the Café de Oriente and the Amparo. But the old standbys, like the Jockey Club, the Zalacaín, Horcher and the Príncipe de Viana are still popular and frequented by old and young alike, and should definitely be experienced for an elegant dinner and a taste of traditional Spain.

Your best sources for information about what is going on in Madrid, day or night, are the local newspaper, one of the numerous activity guides available at street kiosks and often found in hotel rooms or, better yet, if you do not read Spanish, the concierge at your hotel, who always seems to know what's up and can make arrangements for you, too - from dinner, to bullfights to flamenco shows.

SIDE TRIPS: El Escorial, Avila and Segovia may be visited in several ways. There are organized bus tours leaving from the Plaza de Oriente early every morning which include visits to all three places in one day. Your hotel can make the arrangements for you, the price is reasonable and the guides speak English. This method, however, is necessarily a rather quick tour of these wonderful towns and gives you very little flexibility. But, if all you want (or have time for) is a quick look, this is probably your best bet.

A better way to go, in our opinion, is to drive yourself. This will allow you to allocate your time as you please. These towns are all close to Madrid and close to each other, so you could fit them all into one long day if you must. But, if you decide you want to spend more than one day seeing them (and they certainly merit it), you will find hotel recommendations for all three towns in *Places to Stay* section.

Head northwest on A6 from Madrid, turning left about 30 kilometers out of town on C600 to reach the MONASTERY OF SAINT LAWRENCE THE ROYAL OF EL ESCORIAL (Monasterio de San Lorenzo el Real de El Escorial), better known as just El Escorial, and one of Spain's most impressive edifices. Built by King Phillip II in the late 16th century, the building was designed to house a church, a monastery, a mausoleum and the palace for the royal family. One of Phillip's main motivations was a promise he had made to dedicate a church to St. Lawrence on the occasion of an important Spanish victory over France which occurred on the feast day of that saint. A second motive was that his father, Charles V, Emperor of the largest empire the world had ever known, had expressed the wish that a proper tomb be erected for him. So when Phillip II moved the capital from Toledo to Madrid in 1559 in order to put it in the center of the country, he began construction of El Escorial on the site of the slag heap (escorial) of some abandoned iron mines. The construction lasted from 1563 to 1584 and resulted in a complex of some 340,000 square feet. Perhaps no other building more faithfully reflects the personality of its owner than this.

Phillip II was a deeply religious man, obsessively so in the opinion of many. (It is perhaps understandable, since he spent most of his life in mourning.   Seventeen of his close relatives died during his lifetime, including all of his sons but one, and his four wives.)   He thus lavished great sums of money on the decoration of the religious parts of the building, while the palace itself was a simple, even austere affair from which Phillip ruled half the world.   Subsequent monarchs added some decorative touches to the apartments or installed additional ones, as in the case of the Bourbon apartments.   The Pantheon of the Kings, directly below the high altar of the church, contains the remains of almost all the Spanish monarchs from Charles V on (with the kings on the left, queens on the right).   The lavishly decorated library contains some 40,000 volumes, and there and elsewhere in the building you will discover examples of the works of all the great painters of the 16th century.   El Escorial elicits varied reactions from visitors: some seeing it as a morose pile of rock with 2,600 too-small windows, others as a totally unique royal monument built by a unique monarch.   There is certainly no denying its interest as a symbol of some important aspects of 16th century Spain.

Head back toward A6 via C600 and watch for a turnoff to the left leading to the VALLE DE LOS CAIDOS (Valley of the Fallen).   This memorial to Spain's Civil War dead is dominated by a 400-foot by 150-foot cross (which has an elevator on the north side) and is the final resting place of Generalísimo Francisco Franco, who ruled Spain from 1939-1975.

Return to the A6 freeway and continue northwest to VILLACASTIN, where you exit to reach AVILA, traversing pretty countryside of rolling hills.   Approached from any direction   Avila is a dramatic sight.   Enclosed by stone walls it stands today as it must have appeared to a potential aggressor in the Middle Ages.   The 11th century fortifications are the oldest and best-preserved in Spain, are one-and-a-half miles long, ten feet thick and average 35 feet in height.   They have nine gates and eighty-eight towers.   A stroll along the sentry path atop the walls affords a close-up view of the many storks nests perched in the towers and rooftops of the city.

Besides the walls being impressive, the fortress-like cathedral is a particularly fine one. Mostly early Gothic in form, it contains some beautiful stained glass and ironwork. The Convento de Santa Teresa, a few blocks southwest of the cathedral, is built on the birthplace of the famous 16th century mystic writer, who is generally credited with defeating the Reformation in Spain by carrying out reforms of her own. Inside there are relics related to the saint and some fine altars. In the immediate vicinity are some lovely and picturesque 15th century houses. You will enjoy strolling around the ancient town, with its tiny plazas and cobbled streets.

Avila Wall

Just outside the walls on the northeast corner is St Vincent's church, founded in 1307. Noteworthy are the Tomb of the Patron Saints (12th century), a crypt with the stone where St. Vincent and his sisters were martyred (in the 4th century), and the west entrance with its rich Romanesque sculpture.

Also outside the walls, via the Puerta del Alcázar gate and across the Plaza de Santa Mariá, is St. Peter's church, with its impressive rose window. To the left is the Calle del Duque de Alba which leads (400 yards) to the Convento de San José, the first convent founded by Santa Teresa and now home to a museum of mementos related to her life.

Besides the Fogón de Santa María, the restaurant in the Hotel Palacio Valderrábanos, which is excellent but somewhat uninspired in decor, another of our favorite restaurants is Mesón el Rastro, an ancient inn built into the walls next to the Puerta del Rastro gate (east of the Santa María gate.) Basic, traditional dishes are served in an atmosphere typical of old Spain, with roast suckling pig (*cochinillo asado*) and the veal chop (*chuletón de Avila*) being two particularly good offerings.

To reach SEGOVIA, return the way you came to the A6 freeway and continue past it on N110. Segovia was an important city even before the Romans came in 80 B.C. It was occupied by the Moors between the 8th and 11th centuries, and was reconquered by the Christians in 1085.

The highlight of Segovia is the 14th century Alcázar castle. Dramatically situated like a ship on the high sea, it is a sight not soon forgotten. This is the castle used in the film "Camelot", from whose ramparts Lancelot launches into the song "*C'est moi*" before crossing the English Channel to join King Arthur's knights of the round table. Probably the most-photographed edifice in Spain, it is quite bare inside. The tour is most memorable for its views. In 1474, Castilian King Henry IV's sister, Isabella, was here proclaimed Queen of Castile (which at that time included most of the western half of Spain and Andalusia), laying the groundwork for the creation of the modern nation, due to her marriage to Ferdinand, heir of Aragón.

Segovia claims one of the finest Roman aqueducts still in existence, and it still functions to bring water from the Riofrío river to the city. Thought to have been built in the first or second century A.D., it is constructed, without mortar, of granite from the nearby mountains. It is almost half a mile long and over 90 feet above the ground at its highest point as it crosses the Plaza de Azoguejo.

A tour around the outside of the city walls to the north affords some excellent perspectives on the setting. Bear left from the aqueduct and you pass the old Moneda (Mint) and the Monasterio del Parral, on the left bank of the Eresma river. After crossing the bridge bear left, then right to the Church of the Vera Cruz, from where you can enjoy a spectacular view of the city. A little farther north is the Convento de Carmelitas Descalzos, where the great mystic poet of the

15th century, St. John of the Cross, is buried. To wind up your sightseeing with more city views, return to town via the Cuesta de los Hoyos.

In the old city are narrow, picturesque streets which deserve a half-day walking tour. The Church of St. Stephen is a lovely Romanesque building from the 13th century. Farther down is the cathedral, said to be the last Gothic cathedral built in Spain. East another block is St. Martin's (12th century), and a couple of blocks farther is one of the most unique mansions in Segovia, the Casa de los Picos. Northwest of there is the Plaza del Conde de Cheste with its numerous palaces. If you head south from here, you will find yourself back where the aqueduct crosses the Plaza del Azoguejo.

You should try not to leave Segovia without eating at either the Mesón de Duque (Cervantes 12) or at the Mesón de Cándido (Azoguejo 5, next to the aqueduct). The Candido is over 100 years old (though the building dates from the 15th century), has whitewashed rooms with beamed ceilings, and offers excellent regional fare and a delightful ambiance. The specialty in both restaurants is *cochinillo asado* (roast suckling pig).

Alcázar Castle
Segovia

Moorish Memories

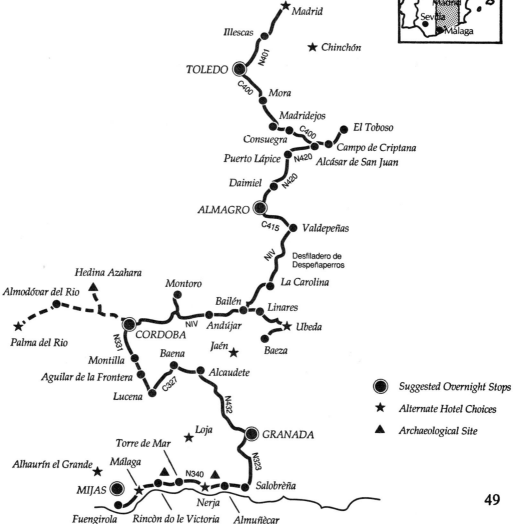

Santiago
Barcelona
Madrid
Sevilla
Málaga

★ Madrid

Illescas

N401

★ Chinchón

TOLEDO

C400

Mora

Madridejos

C400

El Toboso

Consuegra

Campo de Criptana

Puerto Lápice

N420

Alcásar de San Juan

Daimiel

N420

ALMAGRO

C415

Valdepeñas

NIV

Desfiladero de
Despeñaperros

La Carolina

Hedina Azahara

Montoro

Almodóvar del Rio

Bailén

Linares

NIV

Andújar

Ubeda

Palma del Rio

N331

CORDOBA

Jaén ★

Baeza

Baena

Montilla

Alcaudete

Aguilar de la Frontera

C327

N432

Lucena

GRANADA

Loja

N323

Torre de Mar

Alhaurín el Grande

Málaga

MIJAS

N340

Salobrèña

Fuengirola

Rincòn do le Victoria

Nerja

Almuñècar

⦿ Suggested Overnight Stops

★ Alternate Hotel Choices

▲ Archaeological Site

49

Moorish Memories

The culture of contemporary Spain is a rich mixture of its prehistoric Celt-Iberian, Roman, Visigothic and Moorish heritage. When the last of the Moors (Moslems) were expelled from Granada in 1492, after almost 800 years of war known as the Reconquest, the modern nation of Spain was born. Each of the cultures left its mark, however, and nowhere is the variety of modern Spain more evident than in the area covered by this itinerary: from cosmopolitan Madrid to the glamorous Costa del Sol, playground of the jet set. You visit historic Toledo, capital of Visigothic Spain from the 6th to the 8th centuries, and of Christian Spain from 1085 to the mid-16th century. Chosen home of the renowned painter, El Greco, Toledo is perhaps the most Spanish of all Spanish towns and a veritable open-air museum of history.

Don Quixote Country

Next you traverse the plains and pass the windmills of La Mancha, wandering ground of Don Quixote, to Córdoba - capital of Moorish Spain and, in the 10th century, second in wealth and luxury only to Baghdad. Córdoba still recalls the glory of the Moslem empire on the peninsula. Next you visit the Moors' last stronghold, Granada, where the most spectacular architectural monument of that culture, the Alhambra, towers majestically over the city. This itinerary ends on the sunny beaches of the Costa del Sol (Coast of the Sun), where European royalty and Hollywood stars moor their yachts.

Your route passes miles of olive groves and vineyards and winds through small towns spilling down mountainsides under the remains of ancient castles. Be sure to sample the regional wines (Valdepeñas), the delicious cold gazpacho soup (there is nothing so refreshing on a hot day) and the varied seafood specialties.

ORIGINATING CITY   MADRID

Whether before or after your stay in Spain's capital city, a journey to her southern cities, steeped in Moorish heritage and graced with Mudejar mementos, should not be missed. So, when you are ready to leave the hustle and bustle of Madrid, head south to follow in the footsteps of Don Quixote and the warriors who reclaimed Spain for the Christians.

DESTINATION I   TOLEDO   Hostal del Cardenal

Take N401 south from Madrid to TOLEDO, passing through the medieval town of ILLESCAS. Fortified Toledo is lovely to come upon, and you may wish to take a turn around the walled city (bear right just before entering the Bisagra gate) when you first arrive.   When you witness the incredible views of the city from the hillside across the Tagus river you will understand what inspired El Greco's famous painting, "View of Toledo" (now in the Prado).

The city itself can be terribly frustrating to drive in, so it is preferable to leave your car outside the city walls and walk the short distance into the city.   The HOSTAL DEL CARDENAL, former summer residence of Cardinal Lorenzana (Archbishop of Toledo in the 18th century), is built into the walls themselves, and just 100 yards from one of the main city gates.   Besides the romance of its historical setting, the convenience of its location and accommodations, it also boasts one of the finest restaurants in town, so you will definitely want to enjoy a leisurely *al fresco comida* in the garden patio (roast pig and lamb are the specialties) after exploring the town.

Sights abound in Toledo.   When the capital was moved to Madrid in the 16th century, Toledo remained the center of the Catholic hierarchy in Spain and the cathedral (13th to 15th centuries) reminds you of the great cathedrals of France, but is even more richly adorned.   In Santo Tomé church you can view El Greco's famous "Burial of the Count of Orgaz" in its original setting (the sixth figure from the left is said to be a self-portrait of the artist), and the El Greco House and museum lends an idea of how he lived.   Also noteworthy is the startling Mudéjar decoration of the El Tránsito and Santa María la Blanca synagogues.   The Santa Cruz Museum, with its fine 16th and 17th century art, includes twenty-two works by El Greco.   But above all, roaming the ancient, winding streets of the city, pausing for refreshment in a pretty town square (such as the Plaza de Zocodover), soaking up the essence of Spanish history, and sitting on the terrace of the parador bar to watch the city turn golden in the setting sun are the highlights of Toledo's offerings.

Toledo is loaded with souvenir shops and famous for its swords and knives - you will find both decorative and real ones in all shapes, sizes and prices - and for its damascene ware: gold, silver and copper filigree inlaid in black steel.

Hostal del Cardenal
Toledo

| DESTINATION II | ALMAGRO | P.N. de Almagro |

Leave Toledo on C400. You will soon be in La Mancha (from manxa, an Arabic word meaning parched earth), the land of Cervantes' Don Quixote, famous for its wine, cheese (*queso manchego*), windmills, saffron, olive trees and ceramics. Above CONSUEGRA, you will pass the romantic sight of a ruined 12th century castle surrounded by thirteen windmills. (The best picture-taking spot is after you leave the town to the east.) Between here and MADRIDEJOS look for *alfares*, the pottery studios for which this area is known.

If you are a Cervantes (or a "Man of La Mancha") fan, you should take the short side trip (about 50 fairly fast kilometers each way) east from Madridejos on C400 toward the wine-trade town of ALCAZAR DE SAN JUAN, which you bypass continuing east to reach CAMPO DE CRIPTANA where, it is claimed, Don Quixote had his tryst with the windmills. A few kilometers farther east will bring you to the Criptana Hermitage at the junction of N420 and TO104, and another splendid view of the countryside dotted with windmills. About 15 kilometers northeast is EL TOBOSO. Just southeast of the church in the center of town is a reproduction of the home of the peerless Dulcinea, reluctant recipient of the knight errant's undying love. The house supposedly belonged to Ana Martínez whom Cervantes renamed Dulcinea (dulce = sweet + Ana). You will enjoy touring the house which contains 17th century furniture and an intriguing antique olive-oil press in the patio in the back. Across the street from the church is a collection of over three-hundred editions of the novel in everything from Japanese to Gaelic. A number of interesting facsimiles, signed, and illuminated editions are housed there, too. If you know some Spanish, you will see that there are signs which are quotations from the novel all around town pointing the way to the church. (Note: On the Michelin map you may see a place to the east of El Toboso called Venta del Quijote - do not bother, it is closed. See below for another, more interesting place by the same name.)

Return to Alcázar de San Juan and from there head for PUERTO LAPICE, where you can follow the signs to the delightful Venta del Quijote - a well-restored example of the type of inn where Don Quixote was dubbed knight. The Venta has a charming restaurant and bar, as well as some cute little shops. Continuing southwest, you pass through the fertile plains of the Campo de Calatrava, on the way to DAIMIEL. Take C417 south to the lovely town of ALMAGRO, once the main stronghold of the knights of the military Order of Calatrava, who battled the Moors during the Reconquest.

Almagro's unique, oblong Plaza Mayor is surrounded by wooden houses, and the restored 16th century Corral de Comedias (in the southeast corner) is where the plays of the Spanish Golden Age were performed. It is similar in style and epoch (as were the plays) to the Elizabethan theaters of Shakespeare's time. You will enjoy exploring the town's cobbled streets and alleyways, with their marvelous whitewashed houses, sculptured doorways and shops selling the renowned, locally tatted lace. A number of other historic buildings are in the process of restoration.

Parador Nacional de Almagro
Almagro

Your hotel is the graceful PARADOR NACIONAL DE ALMAGRO, installed in a 16th century convent, whose Moorish arches, patios and musical fountains will prepare you for tomorrow's entrance into the delights of Andalusia. The building is mostly new, but the manager says he has trouble convincing people of that because of the incredible attention to detail in the re-creation of the original.

As a sidetrip from Almagro, is a visit of the wine center of VALDEPEÑAS, a short drive to the east. As you leave Almagro you are likely to see women outside their homes bent over their work of lace-making. After a short drive through vine-laden flatland, you will arrive in Valdepeñas, which has made a name for itself with its good light table wine. Its largest winery, the Invencible Cooperative Winestore (watch for it on your left just after you cross the railroad tracks at the edge of town), which processes the grapes of eight hundred and fifty growers, is open to visitors and well worth a stop for a taste or two, especially of the light red. Wine-harvest festivals are held here in September. Valdepeñas has a charming central plaza, and the Victory Monument hill north of the town on NIV offers a splendid panorama of vine-covered plains. Another worthwhile sidetrip from Almagro is 21 kilometers southwest where, outside the town of Calzada de Calatrava, are the fascinating ruins of the 13th century castle of Calatrava la Nueva.

DESTINATION III	CORDOBA	Hotel Maimónides

When you are ready to leave Almagro, regain NIV and head south, climbing gradually into the pine-forested Sierra Morena until, at the Despeñaperros gorge (*despeña perros* = throwing off of the dogs, i.e. Moors), you officially enter Andalusia. The Andalusians are fond of saying that this is where Europe ends and Africa begins. This is not a total exaggeration - Andalusia has a markedly different culture and a much stronger Moorish tradition than the rest of Spain.

You will pass through LA CAROLINA before coming to BAILEN, where you head east on N322 through LINARES to UBEDA. Recaptured from the Moors in 1234, it once served as an important base in the Reconquest campaign. The heart of all Spanish towns is the plaza, and Ubeda's striking oblong Plaza Vázquez de Molina was designed for lingering, lined with palaces and mansions with classic Renaissance façades, grills and balconies and the beautiful El Salvador chapel. You can also spot the remains of old town walls and towers around town. Ubeda's elegant parador (on the plaza in a 16th century palace) offers an imaginative lunch menu, if the time is appropriate.

From Ubeda it's a short drive to captivating BAEZA, the seat of a bishop during the Visigothic period and a prominent border town between Andalusia and La Mancha during the Reconquest. Golden seignorial mansions testify to its importance as a Moorish capital before 1227, when it became the first Andalusian town to be reconquered. Make time to drop by the tourist office in the enchanting Plaza de los Leones, pick up a town map, and wander on foot from there to visit this open-air museum of architecture, dating from Romanesque through Renaissance.

Return to Bailen, then head west toward CORDOBA. You will pass ANDUJAR, with a pretty little plaza dominated by an ochre-colored Gothic church, and an arched Roman bridge across the Guadalquivir. You are in the major olive-producing region of Spain now, and will drive by seemingly unending, symmetrical rows of olive trees (olivos). After passing VILLA DEL RIO, on the left bank of the river is the fortified town of MONTORO just off the main road to the north. This was an important stronghold during the Moorish period, and you may wish to take time to wander across the 14th century bridge to the old town and explore its picturesque Andalusian streets. The remaining 55 kilometers to Córdoba passes through a sea of olivos parted occasionally by cotton fields.

Córdoba was the most opulent of the Moorish cities in Spain and boasted a university to which scholars from all over Europe came to study in the 11th and 12th centuries, when it was the largest city in Europe. Most of the former opulence is gone, but the city preserves one of the architectural marvels of that period, the Mosque (Mezquita). A vast square of apparently endless red-and-white-striped arches, with a second level above the first to provide a feeling of openness, it is a fantastic example of Moslem construction. The only discordant note is the 16th century cathedral carved out of the middle of it. Even though the Emperor Charles V had approved the idea, he is said to have lamented "the destruction of something unique to build something commonplace" when he saw the result.

Just northwest of the Mosque is the old Jewish Quarter (Barrio de la Judería), a virtual maze of twisting streets, modern and ancient shops, and colorful bars and cafes, often punctuated at night by the intricate rhythms of spontaneous flamenco dancing. This area should not be entered by car. Even on foot, it is very easy to lose your sense of direction in the tiny streets as each one begins to look like the rest. This is especially true if you allow darkness to catch you - which you should do if possible, since the area takes on a very different, magical aspect when lit by its quaint lanterns.

Hotel Maimónides
Córdoba

Fortunately, your hotel, the MAIMONIDES, is across the street from the Mosque. It is most easily reached from the riverside drive, where you go to the right around the Mezquita and then left straight to the entrance. Leave your car in the underground parking garage next door and wander the area on foot from there. Also just across the street from the hotel is El Caballo Rojo, a restaurant justifiably well-known for its cuisine and ambiance. For an interesting variation on the gazpacho theme, try the *gazpacho de almendras* (almonds), made with sliced almonds and raisins. Besides the Mosque and the Jewish Quarter, Córdoba is best-known today for its leatherwork and its native sons, bullfighters Manolete and El Cordobés.

If time permits, a sidetrip to MEDINA AZAHARA (watch for signs off C431 west of town) would prove interesting. In 936, Moorish King Abdu'r Rahman III began construction of an immense palace on three terraces (mosque, gardens, then the alcázar at the top) of a hillside outside Córdoba, and named it after his favorite wife, Azahara. It took decades to complete the sophisticated project, and it was sacked and destroyed by Berbers shortly thereafter. But today, thanks to careful excavation and restoration, the delightful palace can be more than just imagined. Not far east on C431 is the tiny town of ALMODOVAR DEL RIO, above which floats one of the most stunning castles in the region.

DESTINATION IV   GRANADA   Alhambra Palace

Today head south out of town on NIV to follow the Wine Road (Ruta del Vino) on a journey to GRANADA at the foot of the Sierra Nevada. At CUESTA DEL ESPINO bear southeast through FERNAN NUÑEZ and MONTEMAYOR - with 18th and 14th century castles, respectively - to MONTILLA, an ancient town perched on two hills. A short time later AGUILAR DE LA FRONTERA appears, an old hilltop town, whose whitewashed octagonal plaza of San José is particularly charming. Before turning northeast to CABRA you will see MONTURQUE, with fragments of its ancient town walls, and LUCENA, a center of Andalusian wine trade, in whose ruined alcázar Boabdil (the last Moorish king in Spain) was once held prisoner. Near Cabra are the ruins of the Castillo de los Condes, and in town is the 7th century San Juan Bautista church, one of the oldest in Andalusia.

Continue northeast on a beautifully scenic stretch of road to BAENA, tiered gracefully on a hillside. In the upper, walled part of town are some wonderful Renaissance mansions. From here you can look forward to a lovely, if not speedy, drive through ALCAUDETE, dominated by a ruined castle, and ALCALA LA

REAL, overseen by the Fort of La Mota, before reaching Granada.

Granada fell to the Moors in 711. After Córdoba was recaptured by the Christians in the 13th century, Granada provided refuge for its Moslem residents under whom it flourished until, in 1492, the city was recaptured by Ferdinand and Isabella, marking the official end to almost eight centuries of Moorish presence in Spain. The Moors' influence can be seen and felt in tonight's lodging, the ALHAMBRA PALACE, with its delicate arches and colorful mosaics. You may be content not to move for a while as you enjoy the magnificent city views from the hotel bar or your own comfortable room. If you walk out the front door of the hotel, turn right and walk one block, you will find one of Granada's best restaurants, the Colombia. Its views are almost as spectacular as those from the hotel and the food ranges from regional dishes to excellent steaks.

If you are ready to jump right into sightseeing, THE place to see in Granada (indeed, one of THE places to see in the world), the Alhambra and its Generalife gardens, are within easy walking distance. Alhambra comes from the Arabic words for "Red Fort" and, though it is red, its somewhat plain exterior belies the richness and elegance of its interior. After your visit to this magical place, we are sure you will agree with the poet Francisco de Icaza who, after experiencing the Alhambra, then seeing a blind beggar, wrote: "*Dale limosna mujer, que no hay en la vida nada como la pena de ser ciego en Granada*," meaning "Give him alms, woman, for there is no greater tragedy in life than to be blind in Granada". Look carefully to see a plaque with this inscription set into the Torre de la Vela on the palace grounds.

Most of the Moorish part (the Alcazar) dates from the 14th century, and the palace of the Emperor Charles V, one of the finest Renaissance structures in Spain, was designed and begun in the 16th century. It now houses a museum of pieces from the Alcázar and a fine-arts collection of religious painting and sculpture.

The magnificent tile-and-plaster geometric decoration is an expression of Moslem art at its zenith.   The stunning patios and gardens with their perfectly symmetrical design will dazzle you as you stroll through the various halls and chambers. Equally appealing are the cool, green gardens of the Generalife, the summer palace.   Countless fountains - now, as then, moved by gravity only - surrounded by sumptuous flower gardens, orange trees and cypresses, testify to a desert culture's appreciation of water.

Several spots on the north side of the grounds offer splendid views of the old Moorish quarter (the Albaicín) across the River Darro, as well as of the city of Granada.   The same is true of the towers of the Alcazaba (fortress), which is the oldest part of the complex.

Try to schedule a nocturnal visit to the Alhambra grounds.   Some nights it is totally illuminated and others only partially (ask at the hotel for the current schedule).   Either way, the experience is unforgettable and dramatically different from a daytime visit.   Also inside the grounds are two good dining spots, the Parador de San Francisco (see the hotel listing) and the Hostal América - the first large and elegant, the second tiny, homey, in an open-air patio and inexpensive.

But your visit to Granada should not end here.   The cathedral, in the center of town, with its adjoining Royal Chapel (Capilla Real) was ordered built by the Catholic monarchs Ferdinand and Isabella for their final resting place and their tombs have been there since it was finished in 1521.   Subsequently, their daughter Juana the Mad and her husband Phillip the Fair, plus Juana's son, Prince Miguel, were buried here.   Juana's other son was Emperor Charles V of the Holy Roman Empire and King of Spain in the 16th century.

The Alcaicería (the old silk market) around the cathedral is now a tourist area full of souvenir shops.   At its west end is Granada's most attractive plaza, Bib-ramblas. It is a marvelous place to sit with a cold Spanish beer ["*una caña*" (cahnya) is a glass and "*un tanque*" (tahnkay) is a mug] and watch the Granadinos (including the many gypsies who live nearby) go about their daily business.   For the Granadinos, as for all Spaniards, this includes plaza-sitting, and for the gypsies includes begging from the plaza-sitters.   On the east side of the Alcaicería is one of the better restaurants in Granada, the Sevilla (at Calle Oficios, 12), decorated in typical Andalusian style and serving regional specialties.   A few other superior restaurants in town are: Carmen de San Miguel (Plaza de Torres Bermejas, 3); Mirador de Morayma (Callejón de las Vascas, 2) and Alacena de las Monjas (Plaza Padre Suárez, 5).

Alhambra Palace
Granada

The old Albaicín quarter retains much of its former flavor.   For an unbelievable view of the Alhambra and Generalife, try the terrace of the Church of St. Nicholas in the Albaicín at sunset, and do not forget your camera.   Though it is something of a walk, we do not recommend that you try to drive into the Albaicín's maze of tiny streets (although an experienced Granadino cabbie can manage it).   Beyond the Albaicín to the east is the gypsy cave-dwelling area called Sacromonte, famous for its gypsy dancing and infamous as a tourist trap.

Moorish Memories

If time permits and you like mountain scenery, you should definitely take the 60-kilometer round trip to the peaks of the Sierra Nevada southeast of the city. An excellent road (at its highest levels, the highest in Europe) winds its way to the winter-sports area of SOLYNIEVE (sun and snow) in the shadow of the two highest mountains on the Iberian Peninsula, the Cerro de Mulhacen (11420 feet) and the Pico de Veleta (11246 feet). (There is a 37 kilometer road that ascends to the summit of Mulhacen and down the other side to PRADO LLANO, but it is open only in early fall.) There is a mountain-lodge parador at Solynieve where you might stop for lunch, though we suggest you time your excursion so you can eat at the Ruta de Veleta (about 6 kilometers from Granada), a colorful Andalusian restaurant, and a local favorite.

DESTINATION V — MIJAS — Hotel Mijas

Leave Granada on N323, which runs south through the wild terrain of the Alpujarras mountains - to which the Moors fled, and from which they launched their futile attempts to retake Granada - to the coast. After about 15 kilometers, you will pass over the Puerto del Suspiro del Moro (Pass of the Moor's Sigh) where, it is said, Boabdil, the last of Granada's Moorish kings, wept as he turned to take a last look at his beloved Granada upon his leavetaking. The contrast in scenery on the Motril road is breathtaking: green valleys, rows of olive and almond trees, and the towering, snowcapped peaks of the Sierra Nevada.

If you get an early start, this scenic detour is well worth the hour or so it adds to the journey: About 40 kilometers from Granada, turn left on C333 and continue to LANJARON, a lovely small spa with mineral springs in a gorgeous mountain setting with a ruined castle perched on a shelf above it. The water is supposed to cure various ailments and is bottled and distributed nationally - if you order mineral water with your meals, you have probably tried it already. Continue on C333 to ORGIVA at the edge of the Alpujarras. This is the area the Moors occupied for more than a century after Granada fell to the Catholic monarchs. In this picturesque little mountain village you will find fine views of the Alpujarras, the Sierra Nevada and the smaller Sierra de la Contraviesa to the south. Leave Orgiva on C333 toward the south and turn right after three kilometers on L451. Thirteen scenic kilometers later, you arrive back at N323 which you follow to the coastal highway N340.

Turn right and you will soon have the pleasure of coming upon SALOBREÑA, a picturesque white-walled village crowning a rocky promontory surrounded by a waving sea of green sugarcane. These *"pueblos blancos"* or "white towns" are typical of the warmer areas of Andalusia and you will see several as you drive along. Park at the edge of the town and stroll up to its partially restored Alcázar to enjoy the splendid view of the surrounding countryside and the Mediterranean. If it is lunch time, continue 3.5 kilometers west and look for the Mesón Durán on the left. Their paella is outstanding and the setting is absolutely spectacular (ask for a table outside on the terrace overlooking the sea).

As you head west from Salobreña there are numerous lookout points with fabulous views of the sea and the beautiful coastline. The road winds along the coast through the small seaside resort of ALMUÑECAR, with its ruined Castillo de San Miguel. A bit farther on, near the village of MARO, are the impressive Nerja caves (Cuevas de Nerja), definitely worth a visit - vast stalactitic caves with prehistoric paintings and evidence of habitation since Paleolithic times. Its archaeological revelations (including parts of Cro-Magnon human skulls) can be seen at the small museum nearby. The caves are efficiently run and offer a cool break from driving. Continuing west you will reach the resort and fishing port of NERJA, known for the Balcón (balcony) de Europa, a terrace-promenade with wonderful views rising high above the sea near the center of the charming little town.

Before reaching the final destination, you pass through the seaside port of TORRE DEL MAR, with its pretty lighthouse, and the village of RINCON DE LA VICTORIA, where another, smaller cave (Cueva del Tesoro) with prehistoric drawings can be visited in a park above town. Unlike the Nerja caves, this one was formed by underground water and presents a quite different impression. The area is popular with local Malagueños for weekend beach excursions. Follow the coast road and you arrive in MALAGA, the birthplace of Pablo Picasso, the provincial capital and one of the oldest Mediterranean ports. The parador in Málaga boasts excellent views of the city and the sea from its perch on top of the hill. Nearby are the ruins of the Moorish Castillo de Gibralfaro with beautiful gardens.

Continue west, bypassing TORREMOLINOS, a flourishing tourist trap full of hotels and highrises, and push on to FUENGIROLA, where the ruins of a 10th century Moorish castle dominate a highpoint above town. On Tuesdays an arts-and-crafts flea market is held in a small plaza near the west end of town. The traffic on this stretch of road between Malaga and Marbella can be a bit tedious, but it is the best way to get to MIJAS. Turn inland at Fuengirola (follow the signs) to reach the sparkling white village of Mijas, a market center for Andalusian crafts such as pottery, basketry and weaving, and therefore an excellent place for souvenir shopping. Just as sparkling white is the quietly elegant HOTEL MIJAS, a wonderful base, with its traditional Andalusian decor and spectacular views of the mountains and the sea from the individual terraces available with many rooms. Facilities for golf, tennis or riding abound in this area, including at the hotel. Or you may prefer to lounge quietly around one of the three pools. Although it is not on the beach, there are several only a few minutes away.

Mijas provides a quiet oasis away from the noisy, congested coastal towns, but is within 20 minutes of all of them. Do not miss seeing the unusual rectangular bullring (Plaza de Toros), and be sure to visit the Carromato de Max (at the top of the central parking area in town), an intriguing museum of miniatures housed in an old railroad car - among many other tiny curiosities (all placed under magnifying glass for easy viewing) it features a sea battle painted on the head of a pin and the

Lord's Prayer written on the edge of a calling card.

If you are traveling with children, you might want to try one (or both) of the two parks near the coast. Tivoli World, a few kilometers inland from BENALMADENA COSTA between Fuengirola and Torremolinos is a fairly fancy amusement park with standard-type rides. Aquapark, near Torremolinos (you probably noticed it from the highway), is a water-oriented amusement area. Both look like fun for children.

Hotel Mijas
Mijas

Andalusian Adventures

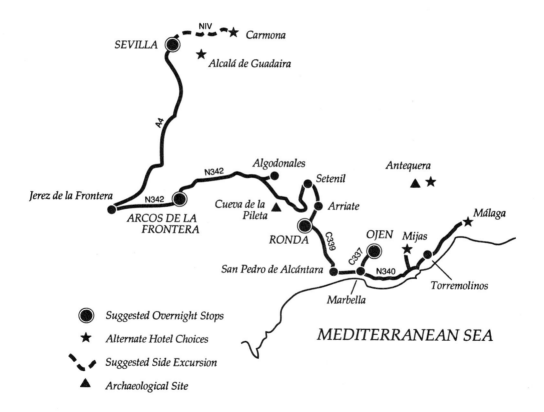

SEVILLA

NIV ★ Carmona

★ Alcalá de Guadaira

A4

Jerez de la Frontera

N342

Algodonales

N342

Setenil

Cueva de la Pileta

Arriate

ARCOS DE LA FRONTERA

RONDA

C339

C337

San Pedro de Alcántara

N340

Antequera

▲ ★

Málaga

★

OJEN

Mijas

★

Torremolinos

Marbella

MEDITERRANEAN SEA

🔘 Suggested Overnight Stops

★ Alternate Hotel Choices

✦ Suggested Side Excursion

▲ Archaeological Site

Andalusian Adventures

This itinerary features western Andalusia, the area that most foreigners picture when they think of Spain, and surely the most often visited by tourists. This part of the region is characterized by the warmth of its people as well as its climate. "Pueblos blancos" or white towns, stepping down hillsides topped by the brooding ruins of ancient castles will become a common, though never commonplace, sight. While this is primarily agricultural and cattle-raising country, the itinerary also includes one of Spain's major metropolitan areas, Seville - the country's fourth-largest city and the scene of "Don Juan", Bizet's "Carmen", Mozart's "Figaro" and glorious 16th century adventures to and from the exotic New World. It also includes the most tourist-intensive area in the country - the Costa del Sol from Málaga to San Pedro de Alcántara.

Antequera

This is the part of Spain that extends to within about 9 miles of the northern tip of Africa and was the first area conquered by the Moors in 711. Except for the relatively small group of Moslems in Granada, Seville was also the last area reconquered by the Christians in the 13th century and it is the area that retains the strongest traces of Moorish culture - not necessarily just architecture - to the present day.

The culinary specialties of the area include gazpacho and fried seafood dishes. Due to the warm climate, sangría is also delightfully ubiquitous. And, of course, this is the home of sherry, whose name comes from the English pronunciation of the wine-producing center of Jerez (formerly spelled Xerez, with the x pronounced sh).

ORIGINATING CITY   MALAGA

MALAGA has seen occupation by the Romans, Visigoths and Moors, before being recaptured by the Catholic monarchs in 1487. It is famous for its Málaga dessert and aperitif wines (sweet Pedro Ximenes, and Dulce and Lágrimas muscatel). Early works of Picasso can be found in the Museo de Bellas Artes on the Calle San Agustín. Explore the cobbled side streets off the main plaza where you can relax at outdoor cafes, and check out the bustling shopping street, Marqués de Larios. From the 14th century ramparts on the nearby Gibralfaro (lighthouse hill) are gorgeous gardens with magnificent views of the town and harbor, and just down from there is the 11th century alcazaba (Moorish fortress). The parador on the hill is a popular place for lunch among locals and tourists alike because of the magnificent views of the countryside and sea from its restaurant. A reservation is usually necessary.

Ahead is a short drive into some of the most attractive natural landscape in Andalusia. Leave Malaga on N340 along the coast (following the signs for CADIZ, among various other destinations) past touristy Torremolinos (which Michener's characters from "The Drifters" would no longer recognize) and Fuengirola before reaching MARBELLA. We suggest you spend some time exploring this chic playground (only about 30 minutes lie between you and your hotel). This is the most aristocratic of the Costa del Sol resorts, with its hidden villas, lavish hotels, long, pebbly beach and the inevitable remains of a Moorish castle. If you like shopping, you will enjoy the many elegant, international shops in the city, and strolling along the main street and side streets is a pleasure. The easiest way is to park along the beach. Numerous restaurants of all types and categories are available here, including La Fonda, with a Michelin star, on the Plaza de Santo Cristo. If you crave more excitement go a few kilometers west to PUERTO BANUS, where the marina harbors enough yachts to rival Monaco or the French Riviera. Unless your yacht is moored there you will have to park in the lot just outside the harbor area proper and walk in. Inside are numerous chic shops, bars and restaurants. There is also a casino there (if you decide to go, in addition to your money, you will need your passport). This is the center of Spain's jet-set scene.

After you have had your fill of the glamour and glitter of the coast, head north out of Marbella on C337 for a spectacular inland drive to the white town of OJEN, known for its anisette-like *aguardiente* (brandy). A few kilometers beyond watch for signs which will lead you off the main road for a five-kilometer drive to the hotel where you will spend the night away from the hustle and bustle of the coast, but within easy reach. The REFUGIO DE JUANAR is built on the foundations of a former palace in the cooler climes of the Sierra Blanca. Suggesting a Spanish villa, its sixteen rooms offer excellent accommodation in a rustic, extremely tranquil mountain setting. You will surely want to have at least one meal here in the handsome dining room which features succulent regional game dishes and attracts many diners from Marbella.

Refugio de Juanar
Ojén

| DESTINATION II | RONDA | Hotel Reina Victoria |

Although Ojén is an unusually peaceful setting, the next destination is the champion white town in Spain. For sheer dramatic setting, RONDA takes the prize.

Return to Marbella, and continue west on the coastal highway to the prettily situated little town of SAN PEDRO DE ALCANTARA, then head northwest on recently improved C339 to Ronda in the bare Andalusian mountains. (Note: If you are planning to visit GIBRALTAR or the Spanish city of CEUTA in North Africa, this would be your departure point from this itinerary, as you would stay on the coastal highway toward ALGECIRAS.)

As you ascend, watch for the numerous little white towns that dot the mountainsides on your left - there are fabulous views all along this gorgeous stretch of road. Ronda is perched dramatically on the edge of the Serranía de Ronda, slashed by 500-foot gorges and cut in two (the old Cuidad through which you enter from the south, and the new Mercadillo) by the Tajo ravine carved by the Guadalevín river (which explains why every other sentence describing the site must necessarily include the word view). Your hotel, the REINA VICTORIA, reminiscent of a white, English country home (indeed, it was formerly British-owned and was a favorite summer stop of residents of Gibraltar), is also perched dramatically on the gorge, making the views breathtaking from any direction. The German poet Rainer Maria Rilke stayed here in 1912-13, which explains the presence of his statue in the rose garden and the memorabilia preserved in room 208 (ask at the desk if you want to see it).

After you have toured the perfectly lovely grounds, and perhaps enjoyed a sangría along with the views from the hotel terrace, stroll south to the Alameda de José Antonio, another fabulous viewpoint, and on to the bullring with its wrought-iron balconies. One of Spain's oldest (1785), it inspired several works by Goya. Francisco Romero, the father of modern bullfighting (he introduced the cape and numerous other so-called classical rules), was born here in 1698. His descendants continued what is still known as the Ronda school of bullfighting. Farther on you will discover the spectacular Puente Nuevo (the 18th century bridge that connects the two parts of town and which you crossed on your way in) with its incredible view of the ravine. When you cross it, you will be in the Ciudad section with its winding streets and old stone palaces. Visit the Plaza de la Ciudad and its church, Santa María la Mayor, whose tower (a former minaret) affords still more picture-perfect views. Some dramatic walking excursions (30 minutes each) can be taken on footpaths leading off the Plaza del Campanillo down to ruined Moorish mills; or look for the foot path to the upper mills which offer spectacular views of a waterfall and the Puente Nuevo. To the left of the Puente Nuevo, (near the Puente Romano, or Roman Bridge) is the Casa del Rey Moro (note the Moorish azulejo plaque in the façade), a lavishly furnished old mansion with terraced gardens and a flight of 365 stairs cut into the living rock and leading to the river and the Moorish baths. The ancient ambiance is hard to beat and invites you to take your time strolling around the lovely streets and plazas.

Hotel Reina Victoria
Ronda

In the newer Mercadillo section of town, Carrera de Espinel is a picturesque, pedestrian-only, shopping street. You will find it running east from near the bullring.

Though Ronda encourages you to stay, you can take comfort in the fact that if there is a more impressive site than the one you are in, it is the one to which you are headed.

Since today's drive is a short one, take time for a leisurely breakfast on the hotel terrace before heading northeast out of town, following the signs to ARRIATE and SETENIL. The latter is a classic little white town with one very interesting aspect - at the bottom of the town, in the ravine, the houses are actually built into the cliff itself. All along this route you will enjoy numerous spectacular views of the mountainous countryside. Leave Setenil in a westerly direction and follow MA486, then MA449, which seem to be taking you back to Ronda. However, on reaching C339, take a right and you'll be back on the road to ARCOS DE LA FRONTERA.

Back on C339, after about six kilometers, you will see a road (MA501) to the left indicating the way to the CUEVA DE LA PILETA. If there are only a small number of tourists at the cave when you visit, you may be allowed to see some of the ancient black-and-red animal drawings found here. The paintings are said to predate those in the famous Altamira Caves and apparently indicate that the caves were inhabited 25,000 years ago. The ceramic remains from the caves are claimed to be the oldest known pottery specimens in Europe.

Wind your way back to C339 and continue west. You are on a road called the "Ruta de los Pueblos Blancos", or white-town route, and you will soon see why as you pass several very picturesque little towns with their whitewashed buildings and red-tile roofs. On the right you'll see MONTECORTO and will have a splendid view of the mountains in front of you. A bit farther, and the town of ZAHARA, with a ruined castle and Arab bridge, will rise to your left. Built on a ridge, it was a stronghold against the kingdom of Granada during the Moorish occupation. If you have time, you might want to stop and savor the atmosphere of either of these classical examples of their type. But you might want to save your time for today's destination - the spellbinding town of Arcos de la Frontera.

(You will notice on this itinerary several towns with the ..."De La Frontera" tag on their names. This means "on the border" and alludes to their status during the Reconquest of Spain from the Moors.) As you approach Arcos you will have several marvelous opportunities to capture its incredible setting on film.

P.N. Casa del Corregidor
Arcos de la Frontera

Arcos clings impossibly to an outcropping of rock with the Guadalete river at its foot. Navigate carefully up its maze of narrow, one-way alleys or you may (as we did once) find yourself backing down those steep, twisty streets in the face of a big truck with traffic being expertly (sort of) directed by amused locals. Since you will be approaching from the north, the route up the hill to the Plaza de España at the heart of the old town on top is fairly easy. Gracing one side of the plaza is a lovely, white (of course) mansion, somewhat austere from the outside, but beautifully decorated within. It is the PARADOR NACIONAL CASA DEL CORREG-IDOR, built in 1966, but managing to reproduce quite handsomely a Renaissance building. And on the other side of the parador is nothing but a crowd-stopping view to the plains below, the full impact of which ought to be absorbed with a sherry at sunset from the terrace - either your own private one or the one off the dining room below. A similarly spectacular view is available from the west side of the plaza in front of the hotel.

Although the view here is the main attraction, you will also want to see the Santa María de la Asunción church on the plaza and wander through the ancient, romantic, winding streets of the old town, where you will get an authentic feel for the physical aspects of life in the Middle Ages.

DESTINATION IV **SEVILLE** Hotel Doña María

==

The next destination is the centerpiece of romantic Spain and, appropriately, has retained its beauty and ambiance even in this modern age. We hope you have managed to leave enough time to enjoy its unsurpassable attractions. Leave Arcos heading west, still on the white-town route, and you will pass rolling hillsides resplendent with sunflowers (if it is summer), numerous typical Andalusian *cortijos*, or ranches, and more dazzling white villages. Then the terrain becomes flatter and the roadside towns less impressive as you approach the famous town of JEREZ DE LA FRONTERA.

The major reason for stopping in Jerez is to visit the bodegas where sherry is made. The interesting tours and tasty samples are well-worth a trip, but most of them are open for visitors only from 9:00AM to 1:00PM, so you should plan your time accordingly. The best-known are Bodega Bobadilla, on the bypass; Bodega Garvey, Guadalete 14; Bodega Gonzalez Byass, María González 12; Bodega Pedro

Domecq, San Ildefonso 3; and Bodega Sandeman, Pizarro 10.   English shippers in the 18th century found sherry wine an alternative to French wine and it still occupies a place of honor in English bars.   The varieties commonly produced here are: *fino* (extra dry, light in color and body), *amontillado* (dry, darker in color and fuller-bodied), *oloroso* (medium, full-bodied and golden) and *dulce* (sweet dessert wine).

Unfortunately, due to the ever-increasing number of interested visitors, some bodegas - including Gonzalez Byass, ph: (56)340000 and Domecq, ph: (56)312507 - have instituted a reservation policy.   To be on the safe side, call ahead as soon as you know when you plan to be in Jerez (or ask for assistance from your hotel desk staff).

The Jerez region is also renowned for quality horse-breeding.   The famous Lippizzaner horses, still used at the Spanish Riding School of Vienna, originally came from this area. For information on equestrian-related events, check with the local tourist office.

If the time of day lends itself to comida (lunch), we can recommend two local seafood restaurants: The Gaitán (Gaitán, 3) and the Venta Antonio (a couple of miles outside of town on C440).   The Venta (open daily) is a large and lively eating establishment, justifiably popular with the locals.   One of their specialties is *Urta a la Roteña* (succulent seabass, peppers, onion and tomato served in a sizzling casserole), whose "specialness" we can vouch for personally.

Time permitting, you might want to consider detouring via C440 to SANLUCAR DE BARRAMEDA on your route today.   Located on the nearby coast, the sherry produced here, called manzanilla, is lent its particular flavor by the sea air.

When you are ready to call it a day and discover what SEVILLE has in store for you, make your way to the A4 toll road, which will take you there in no time.   From the outskirts, follow the signs indicating *centro ciudad*, while keeping your eye on the skyline's most outstanding landmark - the towering golden spire of the Giralda, attached to the magnificent cathedral - because, if you can find it, you can find the DONA MARIA, a special hotel in the heart of Andalusia's capital. Hopefully, you'll secure parking either in the Plaza Virgen de los Reyes directly behind the cathedral, or in the nearby Plaza de Triunfo. Otherwise, we suggest you double-park long enough to announce your arrival and deposit your luggage, then go find a spot to leave your vehicle for the duration of your stay. There are a couple of underground garages within easy walking distance (ask at the hotel).

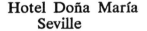

Hotel Doña María
Seville

Seville Highlights

We should preface this section highlighting Seville with a frank admission of prejudice. It is our favorite city in our favorite country, chock-full of fond memories of good times and good friends. Every time we return we fall under Seville's spell - and it won't surprise us a bit if you're enchanted, too. It is not that Seville is totally different from other Spanish cities, it is just that the town and its inhabitants are the quintessence of Spain. We strongly suggest several days in Seville. You need time to see its many sights, as well as time to wander the orange-tree-lined streets and soak up the special feeling that the city imparts to its guests.

The Cathedral and Giralda
Seville

The major sights surround your hotel. The cathedral, one of the largest Gothic churches in the world, ranking in size with St. Peter's in Rome and St. Paul's in London, was constructed between 1402 and 1506 on the site of a mosque. In the elaborate Royal Chapel at the east end is buried Alfonso X "the Wise," one of Spain's most brilliant medieval monarchs, who supervised the codification of existing Roman law in the 13th century. When his son Sancho rebelled, Seville remained loyal to Alfonso. Alfonso's gratified statement *"No me ha dejado"* ("It has not deserted me") is the basis for the rebus symbol you are bound to notice painted and carved all over the city: a double knot (called a *"madeja"*) between the syllables *"NO"* and *"DO"*, thus producing *"No madeja do"* which is pronounced approximately the same as *"No me ha dejado"*. Ferdinand III, later St. Ferdinand, who freed Seville from Moorish domination, is buried in a silver shrine in front of the altar. On one side, in an ornate mausoleum, is one of the tombs of Christopher Columbus (the other is in Santo Domingo in the Caribbean - both cities claim to have his real remains).

Just outside the east entrance to the cathedral is the best-known of Seville's architectural sights, the Giralda. Originally it was the mosque's minaret and was retained when the church was built. Be sure to enter and ascend the ramp up the 230-foot spire (stairs were not used in order to allow horses access). The view of the city is outstanding, especially in the late afternoon. The name means weather vane and refers to the weather vane on the top, which was added in the 16th century.

On the opposite side of the cathedral from the Giralda is an impressive Renaissance building - originally built to be a customhouse but later converted into the Archives of the Indies - into which were put most of the documents (comprised of some 86,000,000 pages spanning 400 years) pertaining to the discovery and conquest of America. Students of colonial Spanish American history still come across undocumented material when they make pilgrimages here for research.

On the north side of the cathedral are streetside cafes which are slightly more tranquil than those along Avenida de la Constitución, and it is a pleasant spot to sit and watch Seville go by.

Alcázar
Seville

To the south of the cathedral is the Alcázar - not as impressive as the Alhambra but a lovely and refreshingly cool spot to spend a hot afternoon. Most of it was restored by King Pedro "the Cruel" (14th century), but he used Moorish architects and thus retained much of its authenticity.

If you leave the Alcazar by way of the southeast corner of the Patio de las Banderas (Flag court) you will be in the old Jewish Quarter, the Barrio de Santa Cruz. Looking something like a set for an opera, this is a mixture of old, typical whitewashed houses and shops - all, it seems, with flowers tumbling from wrought-iron windows and balconies. The painter Murillo (17th century) is buried in the Plaza de Santa Cruz and the house where he died is in the nearby Plaza de Alfaro. Southeast of these two plazas and hugging the Alcazar walls are the lovely Murillo Gardens (Jardines de Murillo), where painters are often engrossed in capturing the setting on canvas. On the Plaza de los Venerables Sacerdotes is the old-world restaurant, Hostería del Laurel, where Don Juan supposedly made his outrageous bets and where you can now have an excellent meal of typical Andalusian specialties. Another excellent restaurant in the Barrio is the Albahaca on the Plaza de Santa Cruz. It is housed in a restored mansion with beautiful tiles and regional decor in its numerous small first-floor dining rooms. (The granddaughter of a well-known Spanish poet still resides on the upper floor.)

North from the cathedral you can stroll a few long blocks down the Avenida de la Constitución to the Plaza de San Francisco behind the city hall (Ayuntamiento), a center of outdoor events during Holy Week. Located in an old mansion at number 10 is a charming restaurant which bears the plaza's name (ring for entrance). The plaza feeds into Calle de las Sierpes at its north end, a bustling pedestrian-only street brimming with boutiques and cafes. Running parallel to Sierpes and out of the Plaza Nueva is Calle Tetuán, another major shopping street.

At the north end of Sierpes, turn left on Calle Alfonso XII, after which a few-blocks' walk will bring you to the Museo de Bellas Artes (Fine Arts Museum), housing one of the most important collections in Spain. There are well-presented paintings of El Greco, Zurbarán, Velázquez and Murillo, among others.

On Calle San Fernando, flanking the handsome Hotel Alfonso XIII, is a golden 18th century building, once a tobacco factory, where Bizet's beautiful and fiery Carmen worked. This is now the University of Seville. Feel free, if it is open, to go in and stroll its wide hallways through the collection of interior patios. Upstairs (to the right of the main entrance) you can find the university bar, where students and faculty convene for a between-class cognac, beer, coffee or sandwich. A visit here will afford you an insight into Spanish academic life.

Behind the university is the entrance to the Parque de María Luisa (laid out by a former princess of Spain), a popular local retreat from the summer heat. Here you'll discover the Plaza de España, a large semi-circle complete with boat rides and tiled niches representing each of the provinces of Spain, where Spanish families like to have their pictures taken in front of their "home-town" plaque. This plaza was constructed for the International Exposition in Seville in 1929, as were several other buildings in the park and as was the Hotel Alfonso XIII. In the Plaza de América, farther down, is the Museo Arqueológico with a very regional collection of Roman antiquities, and an arts and crafts museum. If you fancy being covered with doves, there is a spot where a lady will sell you some seeds which, when held out in your hand, will attract dozens of the white birds to perch greedily on your arms, shoulders and head, and makes a fun picture to take home. There are also, of course, numerous spots to sit and people-watch.

Be sure to save one evening meal for the Restaurante Río Grande, on Calle Betis across the river via the San Telmo bridge. Besides enjoying excellent food, you can dine on the terrace and gaze across the river at old Seville on the opposite bank, illuminated by golden light. The crenellated twelve-sided Torre del Oro (close to the water's edge) was formerly a Moorish defensive tower and now houses a maritme museum and aquarium. Or, if you are in the mood for lighter fare, right next door is a tapa bar with a terrace offering the same view for a smaller investment. Another lively area at night lies to the river side of Avenida de la Constitución, toward your hotel from the Plaza de San Francisco. This is where students gather to eat *tapas*, drink wine, listen to music, dance, sing and converse. The phrase *"tomar una copa"* (to have a drink) implies all or any of the above activities for any Spaniard and often lasts well into the morning hours.

The major festivals in Seville are Holy Week and the Feria (Fair) de Sevilla (about the second week after Easter). Although both are absolutely spectacular events, do not dream of securing a hotel reservation unless you plan a year in advance. And be aware that things can get pretty wild during the ten days of the Feria.

A more somber observation, but one we feel compelled to mention, is Seville's crime rate - perhaps the worst in Spain. High unemployment has led to a large increase in thefts and robberies in the city. Some extra precautions should be taken. Leave nothing in your car, ever. Take extra care of your wallets and purses, even in broad daylight and on the busiest streets. When you are in your car keep your valuables out of sight and be careful at stop lights. A popular local tactic is to ride up to stopped cars on a motorcycle, reach through (or even break) a window and grab whatever is within reach. Unless you have experienced car robbery and attempted purse-snatching, you have no idea how fast it can be accomplished. Be wary of groups of youths on foot and on mopeds, especially on deserted streets. Take taxis when you are out late at night (as you almost inevitably will be). Local residents report that the situation has improved considerably in the last couple of years, but local officials still encourage tourists to be very cautious.

If time allows, there are several good sidetrips from Seville:

CARMONA: Head northeast out of town on NIV through fertile hills to the ancient town of Carmona (38 kilometers), which still retains some of its ramparts and much of its old-world ambience. The Puerta de Sevilla, a curious architectural blend of Roman and Moorish, opens onto the old town, where whitewashed alleyways and stone gateways lead to private patios of what were once noble mansions. The plaza is lined with 17th and 18th century houses. In the patio of the town hall (Calle San Salvador) there is a large Roman mosaic. Stroll down the nearby Calle Santa Maria de Gracia to the Puerta de Cordoba (built into the Roman wall in the 17th century diametrically opposite the Puerta de Sevilla) for a lovely view over a golden plain of wheatfields. There is a wonderful parador here (see the hotel listing) built in the style of an Andalusian villa and blending into the ruins of the medieval castle of Pedro the Cruel. It is worth visiting, and would make a good lunch stop, if the time is appropriate.

ITALICA: Just 10 kilometers out of Seville on N630, a little past the town of SANTIPONCE, is the Roman town of Italica, founded in 205 B.C. by Scipio Africanus and birthplace of Emperors Trajan and Hadrian. Still being excavated and restored, its baths, mosaics and amphitheater are interesting and well-worth the short drive (especially if you will not get the chance to visit the incredibly impressive Roman ruins at Mérida).   If you make the excursion, plan it to coincide with the lunch hour so you can sample the fare at Ventorillo Canario, a simple restaurant across from the ruins specializing in beef.   Mesón Gregorio is another good possibility.   Open-air dramatic performances are occasionally given in the amphitheater here (check with the tourist office on Avenida de la Constitución in Seville for a schedule if you are interested).

JEREZ DE LA FRONTERA: If you have not yet gone sherry-tasting in Jerez, the sherry capital of the world, it is easily visited from Seville, being just a quick 67 kilometers south on the freeway (see the description in the *Andalusian Adventures* itinerary).

The Church at
Jerez de la Frontera

Merida

Cradle of the Conquistadors

SALAMANCA

Alba de Tormes

Fresno Alhándiga

C510

La Alberca

C515

Béjar

N630

Yuste

Jarandilla de la Vera

Plasencia

C501

Cuacos

Navalmoral de la Mata

NV

OROPESA

Talavera de la Reina

El Puente del Arzobispo

Cáceres

TRUJILLO

GUADALUPE

N521

N524

C401

C401

Puerto de San Vicente

Zorita

Logrosán

N630

MERIDA

Zafra

N630

Aracena

Santa Olalla del Cala

N433

Zufre

N630

Ruinas de Italica

Santiponce

Sevilla

Carmona

Alcalá de Guadaira

PORTUGAL

Santiago

Barcelona

Madrid

Sevilla

Málaga

Suggested Overnight Stops

★ **Alternate Hotel Choices**

- - **Suggested Side Excursion**

▲ **Archaeological Site**

87

Cradle of the Conquistadors

Most of this itinerary finds you in Extremadura - a part of Spain less frequented by tourists, which is part of its appeal. The name originated during the Reconquest period and referred to the "land beyond the river Duero" (which runs across the country from Soria to Valladolid to Zamora). Historically somewhat at the periphery of national life, and less privileged economically, the area was rich in young men eager to seek their fortunes in the New World, as the name of this itinerary suggests. Some Extremadurans you may recognize are: Hernán Cortés, the conqueror of Mexico; Francisco Pizarro, the conqueror of Peru; Orellano, explorer of the Amazon; and Balboa, discoverer of the Pacific Ocean.

Guadalupe

Indeed, since the explorations were sponsored by Queen Isabella of Castile, which included Extremadura, only Castilians were given the opportunity to make the journey to the New World during the 16th century. The area is resplendent with fine old mansions built with the treasures found in Mexico and Peru.

Typical cuisine of Extremadura includes one of our favorite Spanish specialties: raw-cured ham (*jamón serrano*), as well as lamb stew (*caldereta de cordero*), fried breadcrumbs with bacon (*migas*), and numerous game dishes such as pheasant (*faisán*) and partridge (*perdiz*). The major local wine is a simple white called Almendralejo.

The last destination brings you into Old Castile and the enchanting medieval university city of Salamanca.

ORIGINATING CITY   SEVILLE

It is never easy to leave Spain's most romantic city but, if you fell under its spell you will probably be back. But Spain offers many additional enchantments and much more of it remains to be seen, so set your sights north.

DESTINATION I   MERIDA   P.N. Via de la Plata

Leave Seville heading west across the bridge and turn north toward MERIDA. After about 24 kilometers look for N433 which will take you northwest to the little hill town of ARACENA, a popular escape from the heat of the Andalusian summer. The Sierra de Aracena, the western part of the Sierra Morena, is known for copper and pyrite production, as well as the justly famous and delicious jamon serrano, which must be sampled - especially if you are a prosciutto-lover. It is a ubiquitous and favorite tapa throughout the country, and you will have more than likely seen the hams hanging from the ceiling of many a Spanish bar. (Enjoy it while you are here, but do not try to take any home with you, as you will not be allowed through U. S. customs with it.)

About halfway between Seville and Aracena is the dazzling white town of CASTILLO DE LAS GUARDAS nestled against a green mountainside. As the drive approaches the pretty town of Aracena, the air gets cooler, the earth redder, and the hills are covered with cork trees. Aracena is tiered up a hillside, dramatically crowned with the 13th century Gothic church of the Knights Templar and the 12th century ruins of a Moorish fort with a beautiful brick mosque tower. Directly beneath the castle, within the hill itself, is the Gruta de las Maravillas (the cave of marvels), hollowed out by underground rivers and an amazing sight to behold. Limpid pools and rivers and an underground lake reflect magnificent and multicolored stalactites and stalagmites. The guided visit takes about 45 minutes, but you may have to wait for a group to form for the tour; if so, wile away the time in the quaint shops around the entrance to the cave which offer a surprisingly good-quality selection of regional ceramic ware.

Heading back the way you came on N433, turn left on C435. You pass beneath the white town of ZUFRE - seemingly accessible only by mountain goat or helicopter - clinging dramatically to the top of a cliff and surrounded by cork trees. Just before you reach N630 watch closely on your left for the ruined castle of SANTA OLALLA DEL CALA, with a white church attached. (This view was one of our favorite surprises this trip.) Turn north to the junction with N432, then left again toward ZAFRA. Zafra preserves one of the most impressive fortified palaces in the region, now the Parador Nacional Hernan Cortés (see the hotel listing), on one of the prettiest little plazas in the area. Actually the former palace of the Duke of Feria, it was the residence of Hernan Cortés just before he embarked for the New World. Its conversion to a parador has not spoiled it in the least, and it's worth a short visit to see the fabulous chapel and the other faithfully restored public rooms. Leave Zafra on N435 and you have quite a fast drive to today's destination - Mérida, caretaker of the richest Roman remains in Spain.

P.N. Vía de la Plata
Mérida

You will find Roman antiquities among those decorating the next hotel, the PARADOR NACIONAL VIA DE LA PLATA, elegantly installed in an old convent which was built on the site of a Roman temple at the top of town. In has also seen duty as a hospital for the plague victims of 1729, and briefly as a jail. The combination of authentic Roman, Arabic and Spanish architectural features (most discovered on the site) within the hotel make it unique, indeed, and interesting to explore. The parador fronts on a plaza where it is practically impossible to park, but you will gratefully discover that the hotel has provided parking in back, next to its pretty mudéjar gardens, as well as underground.

Founded in 25 B.C., the Roman town of Emerita Augusta, now MERIDA, was so well-situated at the junction of major Roman roads that it was soon made the capital of Lusitania. Numerous Roman remains dot the city: bridges, temples, a theater built by Agrippa in the 1st century B.C., seating over 5,000 (if you are here in late June or early July check at the hotel to see if the Classical Theater Festival is offering live performances), an arena (1st century B.C., with a seating capacity of 14,000), a racecourse and two aqueducts, all attesting to its historical importance under Roman occupation. Be sure to also see the Casa Romana del Anfiteatro (1st century A.D. with mosaics and water pipes) and the Alcazaba at the city end of the Roman bridge (built by the Moors in the 9th century).

If your time and archaeological knowledge is limited, you might want to arrange for a guide who can take you to all the interesting places more efficiently than you can do it on your own. Inquire at your hotel (whose assistant manager is an expert guide), the Teatro Romano, or the tourist office for information. And try not to miss visiting the new Museo Nacional de Arte Romano located next to the amphitheater.

A few blocks southeast of the parador you will find the Plaza de España, Mérida's main center of activity. It is a wonderful place to sit with a drink at one of the outdoor cafes, or on the charming, shady terrace of the Hotel Emperatriz, and watch the world go by.

DESTINATION II   TRUJILLO   P.N. de Trujillo

Today's route includes a visit to one of the most fascinating cities of the region and ends up in another. Head north out of Mérida toward CACERES. Shortly before reaching the golden city, keep your eyes open for some terrific castle ruins on your right. Soon after is Cáceres, the second largest city in Extremadura and a national monument. For medieval atmosphere, the totally walled-in section called "Old Cáceres" (also called the Barrio Monumental) has few equals in all of Spain. Cáceres was hotly disputed during civil wars between Castile, León and

Extremadura, which explains its extraordinary fortifications. Incredibly well-preserved, the walls are mostly of Moorish construction, although they were built on and incorporated bits of previous Roman walls. Tradition has it that the most glorious of the military orders in Spain, the Knights of St. James (Santiago) was founded here and for centuries Cáceres was renowned for the number of knights in residence. Many of the mansions were built in the 16th century with money brought back by the conquistadors from the American colonies.

A few hours wandering the winding, stepped streets and visiting a museum or two will richly reward the effort. You can park in the Plaza del General Mola (also known as the Plaza Mayor) where the main entrance gate is. To the right of the largest of the dozen remaining wall towers (called the Bujaco tower), you enter through the Arco de la Estrella (Star Arch). The many handsome family mansions testify to the austere mood of the 15th and 16th centuries. None has much decoration save the family escutcheons which are mounted above the doors - silent testimony to the nobility of the residents.

As you walk along the narrow streets which often lead into small, light-filled plazas, do not forget to look up at the church towers where you will often see storks nesting precariously above the rooftops. The important thing, though, is to sample the ambience of this truly medieval Spanish city.

When you are ready to move on, head east on N521 to the most famous cradle of conquistadors, TRUJILLO, today's destination. Its most famous sons were the Pizarro brothers, ingenious and tumultuous conquerors of the Inca Empire in Peru in the middle of the 16th century. The quantities of gold and silver mined there and shipped home in just fifty years created chaos in the economy of all of Europe.

Your hotel is the PARADOR NACIONAL DE TRUJILLO, which is installed in the former Convent of Santa Clara. A recent addition to the parador chain (opened in 1985), it occupies a building dating back 400 years. Its former residents were cloistered nuns who now occupy a smaller convent nearby. Because they sold sweets as a means of support, next to the entrance of the parador you will see a *"torno"*, a sort of revolving shelf, which allowed them to send the product out and bring the money in while obviating visual contact with the customer.

P.N. de Trujillo
Trujillo

Trujillo also boasts a number of splendid mansions constructed with the booty of the travelers to the Americas. Most of the old quarter centers around the spectacularly beautiful Plaza Mayor where there is a large statue of Pizarro. The irregular shape and different levels of the plaza make it one of the most charming and appealing in the country. On the plaza, among the many monumental buildings, is the Palace of Hernando Pizarro. The mansions here are a bit later than those of Cáceres and thus are not quite so austere. The Church of Santa María la Mayor, a block off the plaza, contains a pantheon of several of Trujillo's illustrious sons. A fairly well-preserved castle towers over the old quarter from behind its granite walls.

The winding, stone streets around the plaza impart an unusual degree of charm and tranquility, inviting you to linger and wander around town.

From Trujillo take C524 south through flat brown countryside dotted with cork trees.   Turn left at the tidy little town of ZORITA toward LOGROSAN, and soon begin to climb into the gray ridges of the Guadalupe mountains.   Twenty kilometers, through mountainous landscape changing from gray to green, takes you over Puerto Llano pass (unmarked) and exposes some fabulous panoramas of the fertile valleys below.   Be on the lookout for the town of GUADALUPE, because your first glimpse of the tiny white village will take your breath away.   Crowned by a golden fortified monastery - which also happens to be your hotel for tonight - it nestles in the shadow of its ancient ramparts.

The Virgin Mary is supposed to have appeared to a humble cattle-herder in this vicinity in 1300 and to have indicated where he should dig to unearth her image. When the pastor arrived home, he discovered his son had died, so he immediately invoked the aid of the Virgin and the boy revived.   He and his friends dug where she had indicated and discovered the famous black image in a cave.   They then built a small sanctuary for her on the spot.   In the 14th century, Alfonso XI had a Hieronymite monastery built there after his victory over the Moors at the Battle of Salado, which he attributed to the Virgin of Guadalupe.   The monastery has been a popular pilgrimage destination ever since, and the Virgin of Guadalupe has come to be one of the most important religious figures in Spain and Spanish America. Columbus named one of the islands in the Caribbean (now French) after her because he had signed the agreement authorizing his expedition in Guadalupe. When he returned from his voyage with six American Indians, they were baptized here.   A short time later, the Virgin appeared again to a Mexican peasant and she became the patron saint of Mexico.

In 1972, the resident Franciscan order officially established an Hospedería (hotel) in the monastery's Gothic cloister (though the monastery has sheltered visiting pilgrims and religious dignitaries for ages). It is a hotel, the EL REAL MONASTERIO, through which you actually need a guided tour. Your stay in this remarkable hotel, filled with antiques of all kinds, will be an incomparable experience.

El Real Monasterio
Guadalupe

When you tour the monastery be sure to see the Camarín, with the image of the Virgin and her 30,000-jewel headdress, the Moorish Cloister with its two stories of graceful arches, and the church with its Zurbarán paintings and many other objects of art.

The positively charming main plaza in Guadalupe has an ancient stone fountain at its center and old mansions huddled around it. Take time to just sit and watch the world go by from this vantage point. As for shopping, this is an area known for ceramics, and Guadalupe is no exception. A local specialty is worked copper and brass.

Cradle of the Conquistadors

If you enjoy ceramics and embroidery, note that this region is the national font for their manufacture (it used to be that you knew where tiles had been made by the colors used), so you might want to do a little shopping along your route today. Even if not, you will enjoy seeing the locals working at their ancient crafts. Return to C401 and turn left toward PUERTO DE SAN VICENTE pass (follow the signs to TALAVERA DE LA REINA). The rocky crests of the Sierra de Guadalupe become sharply pronounced on the approach to the pass. As you drive through the tiny villages beyond, you are likely to spot women sitting outside their homes embroidering (if it is summer). Bear left to LA ESTRELLA, and EL PUENTE DEL ARZOBISPO, a traditional ceramics center with many shops. The graceful old hump-backed bridge that takes you across the River Tagus (Tajo) dates from the 14th century. You will see a beautiful hermitage on your right as you leave town. From here it is a quick hop to OROPESA and your marvelous hotel, the PARADOR NACIONAL VIRREY TOLEDO, installed in a 15th century castle/palace and birthplace of Don Francisco de Toledo, one of the early Viceroys of Peru. In addition, the management proudly boasts a dining room which is a cut above the normally fine parador standard. They host a Spanish cooking school here for culinary afficionados and have a small classroom next to the kitchen.

The small quiet village, spilling down the hillside below the castle, is noted for its embroidery, and has retained a captivating medieval flavor and numbers of handsome noble homes. You will find many opportunities to buy local products both here and in nearby LAGARTERA. You will also be treated to some wonderful panoramic views of the valley of the Tagus and the Gredos mountain range.

P.N. Virrey Toledo
Oropesa

Just east of Oropesa is the ancient ceramics center of Talavera de la Reina, where there are many ceramic shops and factories. If you are still scouting for ceramics, your needs are sure to be satisfied here. The best shops are near the west end of town on the road from Oropesa. (Talavera was traditionally known for its blue tile, while Puente del Arzobispo was recognized by its green tile, but this distinction is no longer strictly observed.) Another interesting stop is the Santa María del Prado sanctuary at the other end of town. Situated in a park, both the sanctuary and the park benches and fountains are decorated with ceramic tiles, some from the 17th century.

DESTINATION V   SALAMANCA   Gran Hotel

When you are ready to depart from Oropesa, return to NV and go west to NAVALMORAL DE LA MATA where you turn north for a pretty drive through rich green tobacco fields dotted with drying sheds to JARANDILLA DE LA

VERA, overlooking the Vera plain.   You might stop for lunch in the 15th century castle which houses the PARADOR NACIONAL CARLOS V and, upon closer inspection, you will discover it to be complete with towers and drawbridge.   It was once owned by the Count of Oropesa, and is where Emperor Charles V resided in 1556-57 while waiting for his apartments to be completed at the monastery of YUSTE, just west of town on C501.   Yuste is famous as the last retreat of Charles V, mentally and physically burned out after more than three decades at the head of the world's greatest empire, and he died here in 1558.   You can visit his small palace and share the view he loved of the surrounding countryside.   It is easy to imagine the serenity he must have found in this solitude near the end of his otherwise stormy life.

Go on to PLASENCIA from Yuste, turning north on N630.   If you have time, we heartily recommend a detour to LA ALBERCA, northwest on C515 beyond BEJAR.   This tiny, isolated town has preserved its historic charm to an unusual degree, and the sight of its picturesque stone houses overhung with timbered balconies richly rewards the effort.   Back on N630, bear right at FRESNO ALHANDIGA onto SA120 to ALBA DE TORMES, dominated by the 16th century Torre de la Armería, the only remnant of a former castle of the Dukes of Alba - among the greatest land barons of their time.   This small town is one of the most popular pilgrimage destinations in Spain because Santa Teresa of Avila, important church reformist and mystic, founded a convent and died here over 400 years ago. In the Carmelite Convent you can visit the cell where she died, and view her relics in a coffer beneath the altar.   Her small, ornate coffin is in a place of honor above the high altar.   And before leaving town, you should peek into the beautiful Mudéjar/Romanesque church of St. John on the central plaza.

Cross the River Tormes and head northwest to SALAMANCA, a picture-perfect Castilian town so special in appearance and rich in history that it is now a national monument.   The GRAN HOTEL is smack in the middle of town and just off what we consider to be the most beautiful plaza in the country.   You will find plenty of old-world charm here - even if the hotel has become a bit worn around the edges -

and the intimate medieval dining room maintains its classical reputation right down to its monogrammed bread.

The most important sights can be reached by walking out the front door of your hotel, and either ahead and to the right into the Plaza Mayor, or straight across the Plaza Poeta Iglesias. Be sure to set time aside to linger in the golden arcaded plaza, undoubtedly one of the most handsome anywhere, with its symmetrical arches and many enticing outdoor cafes. One reason for its beauty is that it was built as a whole in the 18th century and is thus highly integrated in design.

If you walk across the plaza in front of the hotel, you will come to the 12th century St. Martin's church. Not far from there, down the Rua Mayor, you will find the Casa de las Conchas (conch shells), a 15th century mansion whose entire façade is covered with carved stone shells, with the motif repeated in the grillwork and elsewhere. At the next corner is the Plaza de Anaya, and beyond on the left are the "New" (16th century) Cathedral and the "Old" (12th century) Cathedral. The former is Gothic, the latter Romanesque with an apparently Byzantine dome which is unique in Western Europe. Both are good examples of their periods and contain many worthy treasures.

Across from the Plaza de Anaya and the cathedrals is the back of the university. Go around to the opposite side to discover the Patio de las Escuelas (Schools) and the entrance. Salamanca's major claim to fame is its university, the first in Spain, founded in 1218 by Alfonso IX de León. By 1254, when Alfonso X "the Wise" established the Law School, Salamanca was declared one of the world's four great universities (along with Paris, Bologna and Oxford). Columbus lectured here, as did San Juan de la Cruz and Antonio de Nebrija. Fray Luis de León, one of Spain's greatest lyric poets, was a faculty member here when he was imprisoned for heresy by the Spanish Inquisition. After five years in prison, he was released and returned to his classroom (which you can still visit). His first words were *"Dicebamus hesterna die..."* "As we were saying yesterday...". In the 20th century Miguel de Unamuno taught here and served as rector. Not to be missed is the

Cradle of the Conquistadors

patio itself with the statue of Fray Luis, and the entrance to the university, perhaps the premier example of Plateresque art in Spain.   Finished in 1529, it serves as an elaborate façade for the basic Gothic edifice.   If you look carefully, you can find a small frog carved into the doorway.   A student pointed it out to us on our last visit, and neither she nor we have the slightest idea why it is there nor what the artist must have had in mind when he included this incongruous subject.

Gran Hotel
Salamanca

If you continue down to the river, you will see the Puente Romano with its twenty-six arches: the nearest half are actually from the 1st century, the others are later reconstructions.   On the bridge you will discover the stone bull which played a devilish part in the original picaresque novel "Lazarillo de Tormes".

102

Pilgrimage to Santiago

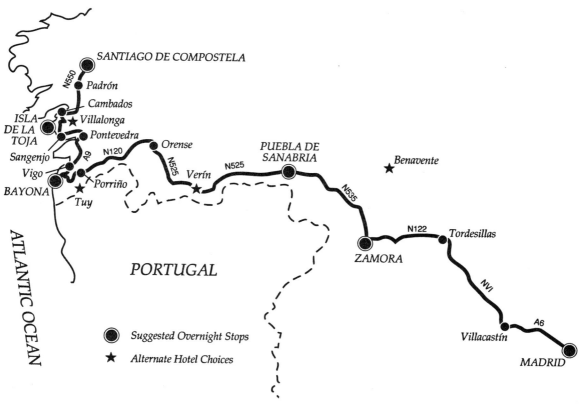

Suggested Overnight Stops

★ Alternate Hotel Choices

Pilgrimage to Santiago

This itinerary takes you to a hallowed spot that was once the most popular destination in Spain - Santiago de Compostela, site of the tomb of St. James the Apostle, and goal of countless religious pilgrims for a millenium.   You will even be staying in one of the places they stayed (modernized a bit since then, of course, and rather more expensive now).   Most of the destinations described are in the region of Galicia: basically, that part of Spain directly north of Portugal (the provinces of Lugo, Pontevedra, La Coruña and Orense).   It was at one time part of Portugal but, as a result of some royal intrigues, was separated from that kingdom in 1128. Although everyone speaks Spanish, Galicia has its own language (somewhat of a mixture of Portuguese and Spanish).

Santiago de Compostela

Because of this, you will notice some spelling variations in town names, depending on whether the Galician or the Castilian spelling is used - we have used Castilian. The area is separated from the rest of the country by several mountain ranges. Perhaps for that reason, Galicia seems to have kept its face turned to the sea and has developed a strong seafaring tradition and economy. It is also the region that has maintained the strongest Celtic influence since the Celts invaded the Peninsula around 3,000 years ago. Galician folk music still has the sound of bagpipes - called here the *"gaita"* - and the name Galicia is from the same root as Gaul and Wales.

Galician cuisine, like that of Portugal, puts a lot of emphasis on cod (*bacalao*) prepared in many ways. *Empanadas* (folded meat or fish pies) are a typical dish, as is *lacón con grelos*, consisting of smoked pork shoulder and turnip greens. Shellfish are also commonly available: be sure to try *vieira* (scallops), a regional specialty prepared in many delicious ways.

ORIGINATING CITY   MADRID

Northwestern Spain is too often foregone by the visitor who views it as relatively inaccessible and has time only for the more well-known tourist attractions. But this region has its share of the best sights in the country and a flavor all its own.

DESTINATION I   ZAMORA   P.N. Condes de Alba y Aliste

Leave Madrid heading northwest on the A6 freeway until it turns into NVI, on which you will continue north toward the first destination. After a few kilometers you pass AREVALO, one of the oldest towns in Castile, in whose 14th century castle Isabella the Catholic spent her early years (she was born in the nearby MADRIGAL DE LAS ALTAS TORRES.) The lovely Plaza de la Villa is typical of Spain, dominated by the Church of St. Martin's two Mudéjar towers. The Convent of St. Francis was founded by the saint himself in 1214. If church architecture is your interest, you should see the beautiful Our Lady of the Lugareta nunnery two kilometers south of town. It constitutes one of the major Romanesque structures in Spain.

Next you come to MEDINA DEL CAMPO, historically a very important Castilian market town, but now not really worth a stop. However, the historic market town of TORDESILLAS, where you cross the Duero, one of Spain's major rivers, does make an interesting stop. Juana the Mad (Ferdinand and Isabella's daughter), locked herself away in the Santa Clara Convent here for 44 years after the death of her husband Phillip the Fair in 1506. The convent has a beautiful patio, and the nearby church has a fabulous artesonado ceiling which you should not miss. This is also the place where the Spanish and Portuguese signed a treaty in 1494 which divided the world between them. Setting a line some one thousand miles west of the Cape Verde Islands, it resulted in Spain's ownership of all of America except Brazil.

From Tordesillas turn west through the small fortified town of TORO - picturesquely situated above the Duero and well-known for its wines - thence to ZAMORA, where you will stay in one of the country's more elaborate paradors. It boasts fantastic tapestries, coats of arms and suits of armor, and has one of the prettiest interior patios in Spain, overlooked by an arcaded stone gallery.

Zamora, which figured prominently in "El Cid", has been a point of contention between various warring factions since the time of the Visigoths. Castile and Portugal battled for possession of the strategic town and it was occupied by first one and then the other in the heyday of the struggle. The fortified town seems to be wall-to-wall churches but, if you can only see one, visit the impressive 12th century cathedral, whose tower dome, ringed by arched windows, should not be missed, and whose museum has a stunning collection of 15th and 16th century Flemish tapestries. The location of the P.N. CONDES DE ALBA Y ALISTE is perfect for exploring the narrow, picturesque streets of the old quarter and it serves as a wonderful base while in Zamora. Although its exterior is rather austere, the interior will charm you.

The town, with its many beautifully preserved Romanesque monuments, is a great place for simply strolling and poking down narrow streets and alleyways. Its wealth of beautiful mansions and quaint little plazas add greatly to the charm and atmosphere.

P.N. Condes de Alba y Aliste
Zamora

DESTINATION II   PUEBLA DE SANABRIA   P.N. Puebla de Sanabria

When you are ready to continue the pilgrimage, head north out of Zamora, then bear left after a bit on N525, which will take you through the Sierra de la Culebra (snake) national reserve. At MOMBUEY watch for the lovely 13th century church - now a national monument. Several mountain ranges converge in the area you will be passing through, forming a gloriously scenic setting. Rustic stone houses with slate roofs and iron or wood balconies are characteristic of this region.

The landscape grows increasingly rugged as you near the magical hilltop village of PUEBLA DE SANABRIA. The P.N. PUEBLA DE SANABRIA here is not impressive from outside, but inside it presents a cozy mountain-lodge atmosphere at harmony with its location.

P.N. Puebla de Sanabria
Puebla de Sanabria

The village across the river is a perfectly charming example of a small Castilian town, including a 15th century castle dominating the countryside and hillside houses from its perch at the top. Do not fail to visit the plaza at the tip top of town. It ranks among the most remarkable we have seen, and perfectly preserves a medieval atmosphere, flanked by hunkering whitewashed houses, the old city hall with its wooden gallery, and a reddish 12th century granite church.   The plaza can be reached by car by crossing the river and bearing left, or, for the hardier among you, on foot from the east side.   Either way you will love the atmosphere and panoramic views from the top.

We also highly recommend an especially scenic side trip less than 20 kilometers to the gorgeous mountain-lake area to the northwest.   The big, blue lake is over 3,000 feet above sea level and surrounded by craggy, green mountains and dotted with small towns.   This is an ideal spot for a picnic outing - you can rent paddle boats (*patines*) if you are feeling adventurous, taking along one of the good local wines for company.   RIBADELAGO, at the far end of the lake (bear left at the fork), is a new town built in the late '50s when floods destroyed the existing town.   It has swimming areas and pretty views, combining to make a refreshing interlude.   If you bear right at the fork, you will climb to the high mountain town of SAN MARTIN DE CASTANEDA, whose wonderful 11th century church overlooks cultivated hillsides dropping to the lake.

DESTINATION III   BAYONA   P.N. Conde de Gondomar

DEVIATION NOTE: If you are planning to head for PORTUGAL, there are two ways to go about it.   The first is to head south from VERIN on C532 to the border crossing and to CHAVES in Portugal.   The other, more common route, is to follow this itinerary as far as PORRIÑO and head south on N550 to the Spanish border town of TUY.   This brings you to the scenic coast of Portugal.   (See the hotel listings for a possibility in Tuy.)

Continuing west from Puebla de Sanabria, you will pass over numerous viaducts with splendid views of the surrounding countryside.   The earth changes from red to white before your eyes, and the hillsides are sprinkled with granite-colored towns. At the 3,000-foot pass of Portillo de la Canda, you officially enter Galicia, characterized by rocky landscape and, it seems, equally rocky buildings constructed from the native stone.

You soon pass the small town of Verin, in the shadow of a magnificent castle surrounded by vine-covered slopes (*viñedos del valle*), and known for its medicinal mineral springs. From there, continue on toward ORENSE, passing between green hillsides dotted with red-roofed stone houses.

The provincial capital of Orense, famed for its sulphur springs, has an enchanting old quarter with twisting, stepped streets overhung by old houses, and delightfully punctuated with picturesque plazas. It was an important capital of the pre-Visigoth Suevi in the 6th and 7th centuries. An old bridge (near the newer one) across the Miño was constructed on the foundations of the Roman bridge in the 13th century. Take time out to stop here to see the Plaza Mayor and its Romanesque Bishop's palace. Park in one of the plazas and walk around the old quarter to visit the shops and have lunch at the Sanmiguel (San Miguel 12).

Continue in the direction of VIGO, passing through the beautiful Miño valley (legend has it that gold existed here, thus the name of Orense from the Spanish *"oro"*, meaning gold). The highway borders landscape carpeted with vineyards and parallels the river Miño as far as VENTOSELA. When you reach the industrial city of PORRIÑO, turn east on PO331 and continue through GONDOMAR and A RAMALLOSA. The road is narrow and winding, but the slow going gives you time to enjoy the incredibly lush forest, interspersed with some spectacular views over the valleys below. At A Ramallosa you turn left and, after a few kilometers, you will come to a bridge (paralleling an ancient Roman bridge on your left) leading into BAYONA, whose former inhabitants were the first to hear the news of the discovery of the New World when the "Pinta" put in here in 1493 (the "Santa María" sought refuge in Lisbon after a storm). Subsequently, it continued to be a major port for the many gold- and silver-laden ships that followed thereafter from America. Thoughts such as these will not seem at all out of place as you stroll on the perfectly preserved sea side battlements which encircle the PARADOR NACIONAL CONDE DE GONDOMAR, your resting spot for tonight situated on this heavenly peninsula.

P.N. Conde de Gondomar
    Bayona

Since you are staying in the premier tourist attraction in town (non-guests of the parador pay for visiting privileges), you will not have to go far to explore the site or enjoy the little inlet beach at the foot of the drive up to the Castillo Monte Real, your hotel.   The castle ramparts are three kilometers in length and parts of them date from the 2nd century B.C. (other parts are as recent as the 17th century). The walk around them affords bird's-eye views of the crashing sea, the picturesque fishing port and the coastline stretching into the horizon.   If you crave more, however, you can venture out to see Bayona's 12th century collegiate church or drive the 30 kilometers down the coast to the Portuguese border.   About halfway you will pass the little fishing village of OYA.   At the end of the road is the port of LA GUARDIA.

Drive from Bayona along the craggy coast to Vigo, situated on the Ría de Vigo (*ria* means inlet or estuary) and the most important fishing port in Spain.   In the 15th and 16th centuries English buccaneers preyed upon Spanish galleons returning here from the rich Spanish colonies - Sir Francis Drake the most famous among them. You will pass some nice beaches south of Vigo, notably ALCABRE, SAMIL and CANIDO.   Though Vigo has become quite industrial, it has managed nonetheless to retain old-world charm.   It surrounds Castro hill, topped with two castles (and a restaurant appropriately called El Castillo), from which there are extensive views of the city and the bay.

Driving in the city is a challenge, particularly as you near the old quarter. Probably the best approach is to drive to the port area, park your car and walk up into the old quarter.   You will find interesting shops and ancient houses in a maze of stone-paved streets in the Berbes fisherman's quarter (which has been declared a national historic monument).   If you are a seafood fan, you will be delighted with the dozens of colorful bars and cafes offering everything from full meals to tapas featuring the day's catch.   Speaking of the day's catch, you will find it in unbelievable variety in the busy fish market (you can find it by the smell) between the Berbes area and the port.

From Vigo head north on the freeway to PONTEVEDRA.   Signs will lead you through town (if you follow them carefully) and out again on the road to ISLA DE LA TOJA (A TOXA in Galician).   You now take a scenic drive along the coast through small resort areas, the inevitable condominium complexes, and quaint fishing villages.   There are many beaches along here, but they are off the road a few hundred yards.   After you round the tip of the peninsula you will see the beautiful four-mile-long LA LANZADA, a gorgeous beach with pale sand and cool, clear water which you will find difficult to resist.   And you need not forego this splendid beach for long, for your hotel is right nearby. You soon cross a pretty stone bridge with tall stone lamposts which connects the idyllic, pine-covered little island of La Toja with the mainland. Here you are going to stay in the world-class resort of the GRAN HOTEL, sumptuous, turn-of-the-century accommodation in an unbeatable setting.

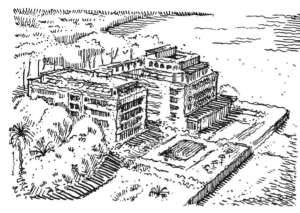

Gran Hotel
Isla de la Toja

This hotel will satisfy just about your every whim. From gambling in the casino to dining in true splendor, your indoor time will be catered in style. Outdoors, there is golf, a splendid pool and tennis. Or you can walk, drive or ride a rented bike to La Lanzada, where you might consider renting horses for a morning ride. This is truly a setting for luxurious relaxation.

DESTINATION V   SANTIAGO DE COMPOSTELA   Los Reyes Católicos

If you have not decided to cancel the rest of your trip so you can spend more time in La Toja, we promise that the next stop will make you glad you completed your pilgrimage.   Cross the bridge, turn left and soon you come to CAMBADOS, whose colorful little Plaza de Fefiñanes is lined with old stone mansions - a good spot to stretch your legs and take some pictures.

Farther on you will join N550 (note the change in letter) and arrive in legendary PADRON where, tradition has it, the boat carrying St. James' remains put in, and in whose parish church you can see the mooring stone upon which the saint's body was placed after the boat docked.   The town was formerly called Ilia Flavia, but *"padrón"* is the word for commemorative stone, hence the name change.

Heading north from Padrón you soon arrive in SANTIAGO DE COMPOSTELA, one of Spain's most famous cities.   Long-touted as one of the finest hotels on the continent, the HOSTAL DE LOS REYES CATOLICOS was built, at the order of Ferdinand and Isabella, as a hospice for the pilgrims who made the arduous journey to this sanctified spot.   Today it lacks nothing to help the modern pilgrim thoroughly enjoy and fondly remember his stay here, surrounded by antiques and catered to in medieval splendor.   Its location on the main plaza makes it a little difficult to reach by car: you come into the plaza from the north, on the east side of the hotel, and drive down a street with a barrier seemingly prohibiting your entry. Enter anyway (slowly), turn right and you will be in front of the hotel.

According to legend, St. James (in Spanish, Santiago or Sant Yago), the Apostle, came to Galicia and spent seven years preaching there during his lifetime.   After he was beheaded in Jerusalem, his disciples brought his remains back to Spain by boat, mooring in Padrón and, after some difficulty, he was finally buried.   Seven centuries later, in 813, mysterious stars appeared in the sky above his grave and led the Bishop Teodomiro to the spot.   The traditional explanation for the name Compostela is that it comes from the Latin "Campus Stellae" or field of stars.   The city which grew up around the area was named Santiago de Compostela, and St. James became the patron saint of all Spain.   From that time pilgrimages began, and continue - although not quite so massive - to the present day.   Most pilgrims from Europe took the Way of St. James through modern-day Vitoria, Burgos and

León.   Another route, considered dangerous because of highwaymen, ran closer to the northern coast.   As many as 2,000,000 pilgrims per year made the exhausting journey in the Middle Ages.

Los Reyes Católicos
Santiago de Compostela

The magnificent Plaza de España (also called the Plaza del Obradoiro) is bordered on the north by your hotel, on the east by the Baroque cathedral, on the south by the Romanesque College of San Jerónimo, and on the west by the neoclassical city hall.   The plaza is without a doubt one of the most majestic in Spain.

The cathedral dates from the 11th to 13th centuries and was built on the site of St. James' tomb (and several earlier churches).   An unusual feature of the building is the existence of plazas on all sides, which allow encompassing views - of the cathedral from the plazas and vice versa.   There is a breathtaking panorama over the red-tiled Santiago rooftops from the upper floor of the cathedral.   Be sure to take a stroll around the cathedral through the Plaza Inmaculada (north), the Plaza de la Quintana (east) and the beautiful Plaza de las Platerías (Silversmiths, on the south side).   Probably the most impressive artistic element of the cathedral is the

Pórtico de la Gloria, just inside the main entrance, where millions of pilgrims have touched the central pillar upon their arrival. A thousand years of loving touches have left the stone worn and smooth. You will discover your hand will fit naturally into a favorite spot on the pillar where millions have touched it before you.

Santiago has one of the most industrious "Tunas" we have ever encountered. The tradition of the "Tuna" dates from the Middle Ages when university students from a single college - such as the medical school - would form a musical group and frequent bars and restaurants singing for their supper. They are characterized by their black medieval costumes consisting of hose, bloomers and capes (each colorful ribbon hanging from their cloaks supposedly comes from a female admirer). You will find tunas in many of the larger cities of Spain, especially in the tourist areas. Today they are more often just strolling musicians who entertain in restaurants and plazas for contributions. The group in Santiago, however, has elaborated the tradition to the point where they not only sing in the plaza but afterwards go around individually, offering their own records and tapes for sale. You are not likely to escape being approached to buy a memento of the experience.

As for the rest of Santiago, most of it can be seen by walking straight out of your hotel, across the plaza, and (on Calle del Franco) into the streets to the south. While Spaniards seem to be able to navigate the streets in an automobile, we strongly recommend that you leave yours in the underground parking lot of the Reyes Católicos (for a small fee per day) and hoof it around the old city. Marvelous old buildings, many small plazas, shops of all kinds and numerous restaurants and cafes line the narrow streets, which should be explored at leisure for a taste of northern-Spanish atmosphere. If you continue about 400 yards down Calle del Franco, you will come to the Paseo de la Herradura, where a calm time can be spent wandering the wooded hill and enjoying in the views back to the city.

SIDE TRIPS: If you need an excuse to extend your stay in the Hostal de los Reyes Católicos, there are some interesting side trips from Santiago.

If quaint fishing villages and gorgeous scenery appeal, get some bread, some smooth Galician San Simón cheese and some slightly sparkling, white ribeiro wine and head west on C543 to NOYA, turning north on C550 to explore the coastal road along the *rías*.

If more history of the Way of St. James intrigues you, drive east on C547 to ARZUA, then on to MELLID - both stops on the medieval pilgrims' route.

If large cities attract you, the major city in Galicia, LA CORUÑA, is only an hour away via the A9 freeway. This was Generalísimo Franco's home town, and, understandably, became an important industrial center during his regime.

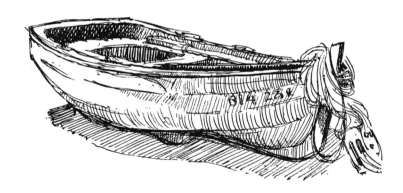

An Horreo

Old Castile and the Cantabrian Coast

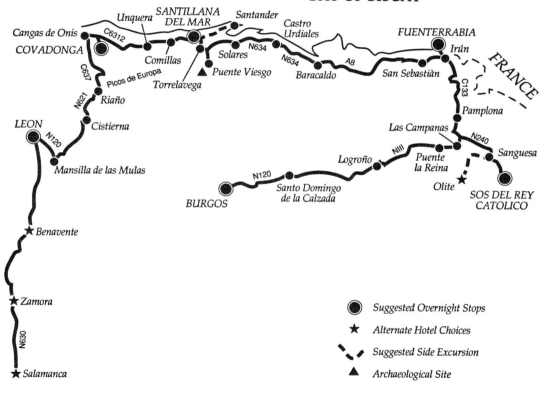

BAY OF BISCAY

Santiago, Barcelona, Madrid, Sevilla, Málaga

Cangas de Onis
COVADONGA
Unquera
SANTILLANA DEL MAR
Santander
Castro Urdiales
FUENTERRABIA
Irún
C6312
Comillas
Solares
N634
N634
A8
San Sebastiàn
FRANCE
C637
Picos de Europa
Puente Viesgo
Baracaldo
C133
N621
Torrelavega
Riaño
Pamplona
LEON
Cistierna
Las Campanas
N240
Sanguesa
N120
Mansilla de las Mulas
Logroño
NIII
Puente la Reina
Olite
SOS DEL REY CATOLICO
N120
Santo Domingo de la Calzada
BURGOS
★ Benavente
★ Zamora
N630
★ Salamanca

⊙ Suggested Overnight Stops
★ Alternate Hotel Choices
▪▪ Suggested Side Excursion
▲ Archaeological Site

Old Castile and the Cantabrian Coast

This itinerary takes you through the north-central section of Spain. Beginning in Old Castile, it includes Asturias, the Basque region, then Navarre (originally Basque, but later "Romanized"), and back to Castile. It features some of the most well-preserved medieval villages in the country and will give you an authentic taste of the Spain of the 11th through the 15th centuries, in addition to amazing you with some of the most spectacular natural landscape on the continent. This is an area filled with ancient cities, even more ancient caves, seaside resorts which are favorites of Spaniards on their summer vacations (because of the cooler climate) and, in the Basque region, Spain's premier cuisine. (The Costa Brava runs a close second). Along the way, you will enjoy some of Europe's best hotels and some of Spain's finest scenery.

Sos del Rey Catolico

The coastal areas of Asturias and the Basque provinces were the only areas to escape Moorish occupation, and it was from there that the Reconquest (led by the legendary Pelayo) began in 718. The region similarly resisted Roman domination and thus retains the most remarkable prehistoric sites to be found in Spain. Castile traces its beginnings to the 9th century when the Christians built fortress-castles to establish and hold their frontier against the Moslems. Soon it was joined with the kingdom of León, and became the major power in the Reconquest, and ultimately in the creation of the modern nation. The Spanish language is still called *"Castellano"*, after Castile. Geographically, the itinerary includes the high central *meseta*, or large mesa, the spectacular Cantabrian mountain range and the coast along the Cantabrian Sea.

ORIGINATING CITY   SALAMANCA

After allowing yourself ample time to sit in the Plaza Mayor and absorb the ambiance of the old university city of Salamanca, head north into the older part of Old Castile: the traditional Spain of castles and earth-colored towns in the vast meseta.

DESTINATION I   LEON   Hotel San Marcos

Leave Salamanca heading north to ZAMORA, on the bank of the Duero river. Drop into the cathedral on the main plaza and take a peek inside the marvelous parador across the square. It is magnificently installed in the 15th century palace of the Counts of Alba and Aliste, and the public rooms are decorated with beautiful tapestries, coats of arms and suits of armor.

Continue north, following the signs for LEON as you bypass BENAVENTE. This 70-kilometer drive is relatively uneventful, but the destination is worth the distance. Upon arriving in León, look for your hotel on the left just after crossing the Bernesga River.

Hostal San Marcos
León

The HOSTAL SAN MARCOS is a pure delight - a luxury parador in a former 16th century convent with period furniture. This world-class hotel occupies a massive stone building with a fantastic Plateresque façade - itself one of the main tourist attractions in the city.

León, now a busy provincial capital, was the heart of the ancient kingdom of the same name and the center of Christian Spain in the early days of the Reconquest. As the Christians drove the Moors ever farther south, León was united with Castile and thereafter began to lose its power and importance.

As is often the case, you are staying in one of the major sights in town - the Convento de San Marcos, with its interesting archaeological museum and justifiably famous 11th century ivory Carrizo Crucifix. The adjoining church and, of course, the public rooms of the hotel itself are extremely impressive.

León is a great pedestrian town so procure a map of the city from the hotel desk and head for the Cathedral Santa María de la Regla, one of the country's outstanding Gothic edifices, and an important stop on the Way of St. James pilgrimage route. It features some of the most fabulous stained-glass windows in all of Europe (hope for a sunny day), which should not be missed. There are one hundred and twenty-five windows of every period since the 13th century, said to total some 1,800 square meters of glass. If you are lucky enough to be there when the choir is practicing, you will have a thrilling experience. North of the cathedral are portions of the old city walls. South of it is the medieval quarter of the city and the small, colorful Plaza Mayor overhung by ancient buildings, mixed with new shops.

An excellent stop for lunch or dinner is the Bodega Regia on the Plaza San Martín, just east of the Plaza Mayor. Owner-manager Marcos Vidal (whose family has run the restaurant for three generations) is justifiably proud of its elaborate, yet typical installation in a lovingly restored 13th century building in the Barrio Húmedo (Wet Quarter, so called because it is where the bars are). From the basement drinking hall to the upper floor dining rooms regional decor abounds. Excellent regional cuisine is plentiful and supervised carefully by Marcos and his wife. The roast suckling pig is outstanding.

| DESTINATION II | CAVADONGA | Hotel Pelayo |

Upon departure from the Hostal San Marcos, take N601 in the direction of VALLADOLID. In the middle of the little town of MANSILLA DE LAS MULAS follow the sign pointing to the left to VILLOMAR and the Picos de Europa and you find yourself on a flat, straight road paralleling the Esla river through numerous quaint little villages. The first glimpse of the sharp, gray Picos de Europa (European Peaks) into which you will soon be climbing appears and beckons as you leave the town of CUBILLAS DE RUEDA.

The Picos de Europa are indeed spectacular. They rise to almost 9,000 feet. within twenty-five kilometers of the coast and provide stark desert-like landscapes which contrast vividly with the humid lowland zone. The Torre de Cerredo is the highest peak at 8,688 feet. The entire range occupies some 1,330 square kilometers of northern Spain. It is a haven for mountain climbing and has very controlled policies on hunting and fishing. Inquire in any of the numerous guide centers in the towns for information about these activities.

In CISTIERNA follow the signs to RIAÑO, and start your ascent into one of the most scenic natural landscapes in Europe. As you leave Riaño, follow the signs to El Puerto (pass) del Pontón. From ESCARO you will be following the Sella river all the way into CANGAS DE ONIS. After reaching the summit of the pass, you will begin the twisting descent, which should be done very carefully and slowly. Soon you pass through the charming mountain village of OSEJA DE SAJAMBRE and, soon after, you will be enveloped by the incredible Desfiladero (gorge) de los Beyos: a dramatic alleyway through the mountains, with the river flowing far beneath you and, towering above you on either side, sheer cliffs broken only by huge slabs of jutting granite. It is like traveling through a scene from a science-fiction movie.

With the gorge behind you, you will come to the quaint little town of Cangas de Onís. Although your destination calls for a right turn, we strongly urge a slight detour to the left. At this end of town there is a beautiful 13th century, hump-backed Roman bridge next to the new one which you cross. A bit farther, on your right, appears the perfectly lovely 12th century monastery of San Pedro. Both merit the short detour. The town itself is also attractive and makes a pleasant stop for lunch.

Hotel Pelayo
Covadonga

Leave Cangas taking C6312 east for a few kilometers before turning right toward COVADONGA. On the approach to town is a breathtaking view on the right of the Romanesque-style Basilica of Our Lady of the Battles, built in the late 19th century. The simple but cozy HOTEL PELAYO (which, befitting its rustic setting, looks like a hunting lodge) is right in the middle of things at the top of the hill.

This tiny town is somewhat touristy but its setting is out of this world, which explains the tourist traffic. The Santa Cueva, just behind the hotel, is dedicated to the Virgin of Battles and is the legendary place where Pelayo initiated the Reconquest of Spain from the Moslems in 718. The religious war raged on and off until 1492. Inside is the famous image of the Virgin of Covadonga, patron saint of Asturias, along with the sarcophagi of Pelayo and several of his relatives. In the treasury are the many gifts presented to the Virgin. Beneath the cave is a small pool, with a spring on one side, where you will see some visitors to the shrine collecting "holy" water.

However, the area's main attraction is reached uphill from Covadonga by a very steep and winding road. About 7 kilometers along is the Mirador (overlook) de la Reina with views of the Sierra de Covalierda and the sea. If you persist about 5 kilometers farther, you will come to Lago Enol and Lago Ercina, crystal-blue mountain lakes in a spellbinding setting in the Montana de Covadonga nature reserve. Though the road is tortuous, it is worth every twist and turn. You pass through green fields strewn with boulders before you reach the icy lakes. At a point called, logically enough, Entre Dos Lagos (Between Two Lakes), both lakes are visible from the top of a hill. This would make a fantastic spot to settle for an afternoon (or a whole day) for a picnic.

DESTINATION III   SANTILLANA DEL MAR   P.N. Gil Blas

In order to reach the next destination, return from Covadonga to N6312, then head east on the north side of the Picos de Europa. Along this stretch of road are numerous, picturesque mountain villages. No apartment blocks around here: the architecture is strictly local. Old stone houses with red-tile roofs and wooden balconies, usually hung with drying garlic and peppers, are the typical sight. You will also start noticing many "*horreos*", or grain-storage sheds, raised above the ground outside the homes.

There are several lookout points along the way to ARENAS DE CABRALES, noted for its blue cheese. Cabrales cheese is made in these mountains from a mixture of cow's, goat's and ewe's milk. If you want to sample some watch for the signs found all along here for "queso de Cabrales". The cheese can also be found in other towns of the area. It has become so popular, however, that "counterfeit" cheese has begun to appear, causing its real manufacturers to put an official seal on the genuine article. You probably will not run into the false cheese here, since this is its place of origin.

From Arenas, the road follows the beautiful, clear Cares river. You soon reach the little town of PANES, where the Cares and Deva rivers meet. Take N621 north and join N634 near UNQUERA where you turn right. You start to see signs announcing the availability of *corbatas*. While this word normally means neckties, in this case it refers to a small pastry folded to resemble a necktie, a specialty of this area. Sample them here or in SANTILLANA DEL MAR.

A brief, scenic drive brings you to SAN VICENTE DE LA BARQUERA, a lovely fishing village where the ocean appears for the first time. You are now on the beautiful Cantabrian coast of Spain. It is a picturesque spot with boats in the harbor and outdoor cafes along the waterfront - inviting if you need a break. At LA REVILLA turn left on the small road C6316 for the short hop through the green Cantabrian countryside to enchanting COMILLAS, a quaint old resort perched above the sea, which was the summer home of the Spanish royal court in the 19th century. It has a pretty beach and some handsome old homes. The large structure overlooking the sea is a seminary.

P.N. Gil Blas
Santillana del Mar

The road now turns slightly inland, through still more beautiful landscapes. As you drive through the village of ORENA, you will be charmed by the little church and cemetery on the hillside overlooking the sea. Shortly afterward you reach enchanting and historic Santillana del Mar, with hunkering stone mansions bearing coats of arms, recalling the lifestyle of Spain's former country nobility. One of these mansions is your hotel. The 400-year-old building which houses the PARADOR NACIONAL GIL BLAS is ideally situated on the main plaza, in the heart of this perfectly preserved medieval jewel.

In Santillana the major attraction is simply atmosphere. It could fairly be called the most picturesque village in Spain. It has retained its harmonious old-world feeling to an uncommon degree. The highly pure Romanesque architecture - from the Collegiate Church to the houses along Calle de las Lindas - will delight and amaze you. Just walk around and soak it in, not being too shy to glance discreetly into the ground-floor patios of the old houses, which occasionally shelter stables or shops. When you leave, you will know at least what it looked like to live in the Middle Ages.

Santillana is not on the ocean, but there is a large beach at SUANCES only 11 kilometers away, and it is only 30 to OYAMBE beach at Comillas.

Another attraction of this area is its rich archaeological heritage. When we were there a large group of American archaeologists were spending ten days based in Santillana to do nothing but visit regional caves. You can get a map (at the hotel) which shows where they are. It is true that the most famous one - the Altamira Cave with its 14,000-year-old paintings of bison and other animals - is practically closed. Its huge number of visitors were damaging the ancient paintings with the large quantities of carbon dioxide they exhaled in the caves every day. Currently, twenty people per day are allowed to visit (though they are studying the possibility of increasing the number), and most of those have either a professional interest or have written months in advance for the privilege. If you write at least six months in advance to the Director del Museo de Altamira, 39330 Santillana del Mar

(Cantabria), you might be able to get on the list. If you do not have permission, check with the *conservador* at the museum in case there have been last-minute cancellations. But do not be too disappointed if not, for there are many more caves - just explore the possibilities.

One example is Las Cuevas del Monte del Castillo at PUENTE VIESGO. Head southeast from Santillana to TORRELAVEGA, then east to VARGAS, where you take the Burgos road to Puente Viesgo. Signs for the caves on the hill above the town can be seen. Discovered in 1903, the caves have drawings some 20,000 to 25,000 years old. There are actually three caves you can visit: the tour (in Spanish only) of the main one takes about 45 minutes; for all three plan on about four hours. They are closed during siesta time.

A fun place to eat in Santillana is the very typical Los Blasones, popular with the locals. It is not gourmet cuisine, but it is hearty and reasonable, plus there is a good chance that *la tuna* (strolling musicians who play for contributions) will pay a visit, adding to the colorful atmosphere. For elegant dining, try the Molino de Puente Arce, about 8 miles west of Santander on N611.

DESTINATION IV   FUENTERRABIA   P.N. El Emperador

When you have finished sampling the unforgettable atmosphere of Santillana, head east toward SANTANDER, a mostly modern provincial capital whose old city was destroyed in 1941 by a tornado and the resulting fires. The road turns south to skirt the bay and continues inland through cultivated farmland to COLINDRES, where you regain sight of the sea. Shortly afterward, you will reach LAREDO, a popular seaside resort with a beautiful, large beach on Santona Bay (with a much larger resort development in the town of SANTONA out on the peninsula). The road again moves away from the coast for a bit, through green rolling hills. You will become aware of how close the Cantabrian range comes to the coast during this stretch.

After passing several small towns with their characteristic red-roofed houses, you reach the picturesque fishing port of CASTRO URDIALES, one of the oldest settlements (Roman) on the Cantabrian coast, and definitely worth a stop to stroll down the pretty and colorful seaside promenade. We recommend you try to get here at lunchtime and stop for a special seafood repast at MESON MARINERO, Correria 23 (2nd floor), right at the end of the promenade, at the foot of the hill with the castle, and just at the edge of the old quarter (park along the promenade and walk). In addition to its local decor and popular ground-floor bar, the seafood is wonderful. We had *gambas al ajillo* (shrimp casserole in garlic butter) and *cantollo* (spider crab), delectable but messy.

Follow signs for BILBAO as you leave town and you will soon enter the Basque Country (Vizcaya), where you will notice a lot of place names indicated in both Basque and Spanish. (Vizcaya's active separatist movement explains the spray paint on the signs deleting the Spanish words and overpainting the Basque.) Unlike the other languages in Spain, Basque is not a "Romance" or "Neo-Latin" language. Indeed, no one is sure where it comes from. Here you will pick up the freeway towards SAN SEBASTIAN, bypassing the industrial city of Bilbao. If you are interested and time permits, take the exit which goes north to GUERNICA Y LUNO, the town bombed by Germans during the Civil War (1937) and immortalized by Picasso in his painting "Guernica" (now housed near the Prado in Madrid). The town has been rebuilt since the bombing, but still serves as a symbol of the brutality of the Civil War, which killed over a million Spaniards when Germany and Russia used it as a testing ground in preparation for World War II.

After you clear San Sebastián (following the signs for IRUN and FRANCIA), watch for the exit for HONDARRIBIA (called FUENTERRABIA in Spanish) and the airport (*aeropuerto*). The road continues 7 kilometers farther before passing under the massive stone gate into Hondarribia.

Your hotel, the PARADOR NACIONAL EL EMPERADOR, is a castle originally built in the 10th century and considerably remodelled in the 16th by the Holy Roman Emperor, Charles V. It has served as host (while a palace) to numerous monarchs in its long history. Reflecting the fact that Fuenterrabía was often coveted by the French because of its strategic position, the castle was constructed with stone walls, six to nine feet thick. When you look out your window through these walls, you really get a feel for what it was like to live in a medieval castle.

P.N. El Emperador
Fuenterrabía

The small, intimate plaza in front of the hotel is unforgettable. Fine, colorfully decorated old mansions with iron or wood balconies with lots of flowers face the hotel on its other sides. The most interesting and charming stroll from your hotel is down the Calle Mayor. The narrow, cobblestoned streets, often too small for anything but pedestrians, impart a feel for life in long-ago times. There is an English country-town atmosphere to the many splendid mansions with their escutcheons in this most picturesque quarter. There are also numerous other small plazas with similarly enchanting buildings.

If you are seeking refreshment and tapas, try the bar on the square, to the left of the parador, called the Bar Antxina; for fine and fancy dining, the Ramon Roteta is a special treat.

Though you almost do not notice it as you approach the hotel, you are only a stone's throw from the ocean. At the north end of the plaza you overlook a very blue and very pretty little port filled with colorful sailboats.

If you feel like a short drive there are superb views to be had on the road along the coast over Mount Jaizkibel to PASAJES DE SAN JUAN. You can stop at the top of the mountain for refreshments at the hostal there where you can enjoy the magnificent views back toward the city.

This is also a good way to get to SAN SEBASTIAN (in Basque, DONOSTIA), a destination you will want to include. This lovely old resort on La Concha bay, with its fabulous beach stretching from Mount Urgull on the northeast to Mount Igueldo on the west has long been a fashionable destination for European tourists. It is fun to explore the area around Mount Urgull, known as the "old" section (in spite of the fact that most of it was destroyed by the British in 1813 and has subsequently been rebuilt). The pretty plazas, winding streets and the many elegant shops, bars and restaurants are lively and appealing, especially at "tapa hour". You will undoubtedly notice the large amount of political grafitti unfortunately defacing practically every exposed surface in San Sebastián. As mentioned earlier, political feelings run high here because it is a center of the Basque separatist movement called ETA, a group responsible for many acts of terrorism (car bombings, political assassinations, etc.). Fortunately, they seldom do such things in their own cities, preferring to make the Madrileños nervous.

The best views are from the other hill, Mount Igueldo. You can either drive up on a toll road or take a cable car from the end of the beach. On top, besides the fantastic views, are an amusement park and a hotel with an uninspired restaurant.

Old Castile and the Cantabrian Coast

However, for a superb lunch (or dinner) continue slightly past the top and partway down the other side to the bonafide, Michelin two-star Akelarre. You will love the fresh fish bisque almost as much as the stunning ocean view and the first-class service in this very elegant restaurant. Try their dry house red from Spain's best wine region, La Rioja, for a sample of how good Spanish wine can be.

(This area is on the border between Spain and France. If a tour of France is in your schedule leave the itinerary here.)

DESTINATION V   SOS DEL REY CATOLICO   P.N. Fernando de Aragón

Your next destination is the birthplace of one of Spain's most famous monarchs, Ferdinand of Aragon. He was a model for Machiavelli in his classic study of governing in the days of monarchy. He was also the husband of Isabella and the two were known as the "Catholic Monarchs" (los Reyes Católicos) because of their strong support of the Church during the time of the Protestant Reformation.

Head south from Fuenterrabía into the lush, green valley of the Bidasoa river toward Pamplona. Along here the river forms the Spanish-French border until you cross the bridge at ENDERLAZA, where the river returns to Spain and you officially enter the region of Navarre. The beautiful, winding stretch of road will take you through the Spanish Pyrenees and numerous quaint little mountain villages with stone-trimmed red-roofed houses sitting in this heavily forested region. SUMBILIA, SANTESTEBAN and ALMANDOZ are all charming towns situated in the midst of magnificent natural scenery. After ORONOZ-MUGAIRE you will wind your way up to the Puerto de Velate pass, through some impressively rugged mountains, then down the valley of the Rio Ulzama into PAMPLONA. Pamplona was the capital of the ancient kingdom of Navarre from the 10th to the 16th centuries, and now is most famous for the "running of the bulls" festival of San Fermín (6-20 July), made famous by Ernest Hemingway's depiction in "The Sun Also Rises", published in Britain as "Fiesta".

If you would rather make Pamplona an excursion from your hotel, you can follow the signs which will lead you around the city and toward the south where you will bear left on N240. Besides the views from the Puerto de Loiti pass, watch for a lookout about 36 kilometers over the Lumbier Defile, a gorge cut by the Irati river through the Sierra de Leyre. The vast fertile valley can be seen for miles in all directions. Bear right to SANGUESA and, just before reaching the town, you see to your right the ruins of ROCAFORTE, a mountain where the people of Sanguesa fled in the face of the Moorish invasion. They later came back and settled in the area where the town is now. Also on your right is a giant paper mill which is the origin of the smell that you cannot fail to have noticed by now, and which certainly discourages a long stay.

You next cross the Aragón river, enter Sanguesa and follow the signs past a 13th century church toward SOS DEL REY CATOLICO, a few kilometers through fields of sunflowers on rolling hills. Just before arriving, you cross the line between Navarre and Aragón. Since Sos is perched atop a hill in the middle of the large flat plain, you will see it long before you arrive. It seems as though it might blend into the brown mountain if it were not for the square tower that juts up above the town. As you get closer you will see that it spills down the hillside under the Sada Palace where Ferdinand the Catholic was born in 1452. The PARADOR NACIONAL FERNANDO DE ARAGON will provide you with a fitting introduction to the town's medieval atmosphere.

Plan some time to walk around the picturesque little village, which is a national monument and has undergone much restoration. You can also tour the Sada Palace and see the very bedroom (or so it is claimed) where Ferdinand was born. There are splendid views of the fertile countryside from the castle and church at the top of the hill.

You might also want to make a short side trip to Javier castle (return to Sanguesa and bear right). It is an 18th century castle built on the site of the birthplace of St. Francis Xavier (1506), one of the early members of the Jesuit order and a very effective missionary to Japan in the service of the Portuguese. If you happen to be there on a Saturday night in the summer you can see a sound and light show.

P.N. Fernando de Aragón
Sos del Rey Católico

Another worthwhile trip is to the town of OLITE (head west from Sanguesa). Passing through beautiful agricultural land with greens and golds predominating, you will also see a number of small, fortified villages clinging to the hillsides. Olite itself is known as the "Gothic city", and you will see why as you approach it from the east. In the center of town is the 15th century fortress of Charles III which now houses the PARADOR NACIONAL PRINCIPE DE VIANA.

Return to N240 via Sanguesa and bear left for about 19 kilometers.   Watch for the signs indicating CAMPANAS and turn left.   At Campanas go south and turn right to PUENTE LA REINA. You pass the Ermita de Eunate hermitage, a Romanesque chapel where pilgrims on the Way of Saint James were ministered to and sheltered.   It was in Puente la Reina that two major French pilgrim roads joined before continuing on to Santiago.   As you leave town notice, on your right, the ancient medieval stone bridge over the Arga river, worn smooth by millions of pilgrims' feet.

Continue west on N111, which was the Way of St. James itself, to ESTELLA where, in the Middle Ages, pilgrims stopped to venerate a statue of the Virgin reportedly found in 1085 by shepherds guided by falling stars.   The Kings of Navarre chose this as their place of residence in the Middle Ages.   Be sure to see the Plaza San Martin with, among many beautiful historic edifices, the 12th century palace of the Kings of Navarre, one of the oldest non-religious buildings in Spain.

As you continue southwest toward the wine center of LOGROÑO, you will pass the 13th century monastery (on your left) at IRACHE and, as you approach TORRES DEL RIO, you will have a splendid view of the late 12th century church towering above the town.   This area is known as La Rioja Alta (Upper Rioja) and, as you will no doubt deduce from the quantity of vineyards, is the major wine-growing region in Spain.   Navigate your way carefully through Logroño, whereafter the vineyards begin to be mixed with wheat and potato fields.

Soon after Logroño is the rampart-encircled SANTO DOMINGO DE LA CALZADA whose impressive, 12th century cathedral has a live rooster and hen in residence in commemoration of a miracle supposed to have occurred when a young pilgrim's innocence was proved by the crowing of an already roasted cock.   (They are replaced each year on May 12th.) On signs leading into town you will see the brief poem summing up the legend, which says, *"Santo Domingo de la Calzada/ cantó la gallina/ después de asada"*. Although the legend says a cock, the poem says a hen was involved. Maybe it just rhymed better. In any case there is one of each in the cathedral. Its 18th century belfry is famed as the prettiest in La Rioja. If you find yourself here at lunchtime try the very atmospheric parador in a former pilgrims' hospice right across the plaza from the cathedral. The saint was a local hermit who took in pilgrims on their way to Santiago.

Landa Palace
Burgos

From here the drive continues through undulating wheat and potato fields to BURGOS. Your hotel is not really in Burgos; it is four kilometers south of town on NI - the highway to Madrid. Since you will probably want to go there first, watch for the signs directing you to NI, which bypasses the city. Be warned, though, that if you go to the HOTEL LANDA PALACE first, you may not want to leave again. The remodelled 14th century castle tower of this stunning hotel will win your heart the moment you enter the wonderful lobby with its carved ceilings and magnificent white staircase. A place fit for a king (and, of course, he and the

Queen stay here when they visit) in the kingly city of Burgos.

It will be hard to leave your lovely hotel but the excursion into Burgos is very worthwhile. The capital of Old Castile from 951 to 1492, when it lost its position to Valladolid, Burgos has strong historical associations with the victorious Reconquest. Spain's epic hero, El Cid Campeador (champion), was born Rodrigo Díaz in nearby VIVAR in 1026. His exploits in regaining Spain from the Moslems were immortalized in the first Spanish epic poem in 1180 and subsequent literary works. He and his wife Ximena are interred in the transept crossing of the cathedral.

The cathedral is without doubt the leading attraction of Burgos. Surpassed in size only by the cathedrals of Seville and Toledo, the flamboyant Gothic structure was begun in 1221 by Ferdinand III (the Saint) and completed in the 16th century. The artworks in the many chapels inside constitute a veritable museum. The two-story cloister contains much stone sculpture of the Spanish Gothic school. Do not fail to walk around the outside to see the marvelous decoration of the various portals.

On the south side of the cathedral, if you walk toward the river, you will pass through the highly ornate city gate called the Santa María arch. After crossing the river, you can continue down Calle Miranda to the Casa de Miranda, an archaeological museum. North of the cathedral you can ascend the hill which harbors castle ruins and affords excellent city views.

Enjoy the pretty pedestrian street along the riverfront, with its shops and lively bars and cafes.

Treasures Off the Beaten Track

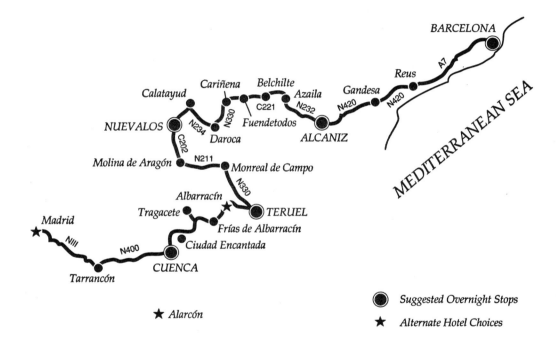

Suggested Overnight Stops

★ Alternate Hotel Choices

Treasures Off the Beaten Track

This itinerary starts off in New Castile, traverses Aragón and winds up in Barcelona, the sophisticated, seaside capital of Catalonia. Most of the route, as its name suggests, takes you to areas not so commonly frequented by foreign tourists, and should appeal to those of you who are anxious for a more intimate taste of Spain. It heads east through New Castile, which holds in store the beautifully rugged Cuenca Range and one of Spain's more enchanting medieval towns, famous for its "hanging houses." Then the route continues on to Aragón with its small, earth-colored, hidden villages nestled in gorgeous, scenic mountain valleys or in the midst of olive groves and vineyards. It is easy to understand why these are considered some of the most ancient settlements in the country: the medieval and Moorish past is evident at every turn.

Cuenca

Starting in the 11th century, Aragón began to expand its dominions and, within three centuries, included parts of southern France, Catalonia, Navarre, all of southeastern Spain, Sicily and Naples. Thus, when Ferdinand II of Aragón married Isabella I of Castile (which included the eastern half of Spain) in 1464, the modern nation state was born. No longer so extensive, the old kingdom is now characterized mostly by agricultural activity.

The final stop, Barcelona, provides considerable contrast: Spain's second largest city and one as glamorous and worldly as any in Europe.

ORIGINATING CITY   MADRID

It is possible to take a freeway most of the way from Madrid to Barcelona; possible but not very interesting. This itinerary outlines a much more engaging way to make the journey from Spain's largest to its second-largest city.

DESTINATION I   CUENCA   Cueva del Fraile

Make your way to the southeast side of Madrid and head out of town on the A3 freeway (which becomes NIII when you depart the city). Continue through ARGANDA DEL REY, then wind through lovely scenery to TARANCON, a little country town with a Gothic church and a mansion built by Queen Maria Cristina. As you drive you get a strong feel for one of Spain's major geographical features, the central meseta, or plateau. The drive east between here and Cuenca is one of the loveliest in Spain - through pretty rolling hills of wheat and sunflowers contrasting with pale, golden hay fields.

Soon after entering CUENCA, watch for signs for the HOTEL CUEVA DEL FRAILE. Follow them as they lead you to the right and out of town. Take the PALOMERA highway (as you leave town, you will get a glimpse of the famous hanging houses), which runs along the banks of the Huécar river. Turn left on the BUENACHE highway for another long kilometer. Installed in a 16th century inn, which has been carefully restored and furnished in beautifully typical Castilian style, the hotel is in the picturesque ravine of the Huécar river.

Cuenca, itself, was originally constructed on the top of the cliff. This is the part known today as the old town, and the area of the most interest to the visitor. The best way to reach this area from the hotel is to turn sharply right just after you cross the river as you head into town. The road climbs steeply and enters a small plaza through a massive stone gate. Park here and walk around the town.

On the main plaza you will find the hanging houses (Casas Colgadas), seemingly perched in midair at the edge of the cliff. Inside one of these ancient structures, in impressive and tasteful surroundings, is Spain's most important museum of abstract art. The extensive collection of Spanish masters is a must to visit. Also situated in one of the old, clifftop houses is the restaurant MESON CASAS COLGADAS. If it is not mealtime, you still might want to stop for a cool drink and to savor the views over the ravine.

Just around the corner from the hanging houses is the pretty and lively Plaza Mayor, with the cathedral at one end and three stone arches at the other. Be sure to save some time for a leisurely walk through the picturesque streets and alleys of this old quarter, and to sit in the lively plaza to soak up the typical Spanish flavor of the town.

The Gothic cathedral, parts of which date from the 13th century, is a national monument: be sure to go in to see the elaborate interior. The treasury is also worth a visit - among other works of art, there are two paintings by El Greco.

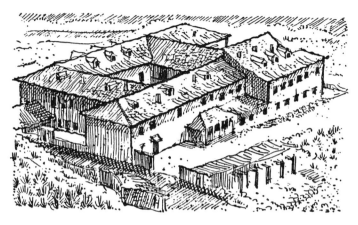

Cueva del Fraile
Cuenca

On the road to the hotel from town, just as you are leaving the city, look up on the cliff on the right side for a whitewashed cave entrance. This is the Cueva del Tío Serafín, a very picturesque bar built completely inside the cave. The little terrace on the cliff affords an excellent view of Cuenca from an unusual vantage point. It is reached by a stairway carved out of the cliff wall.

DESTINATION II   TERUEL   P.N. de Teruel

When you are ready to leave, return to Cuenca, and then head north on CU921 through the Júcar river ravine (Hoz). Take the turnoff toward VALDECABRAS for a gorgeous drive through rugged mountain terrain to the CIUDAD

ENCANTADA (Enchanted City).   This eerie scene has been created by wind and water erosion which has separated large rock formations from their surrounding mass and carved them into shapes which resemble, with a bit of imagination, buildings, animals and monsters.   You buy your ticket from the booth and follow a well-marked footpath for about an hour through the interesting rock formations. The tour makes a cool and refreshing break from driving.

Continue on the same road, passing through UNA and LA TOBA, at the end of a lovely turquoise reservoir surrounded by green pines. Follow the meandering Júcar river, then the signs to Teruel, climbing through the Puerto de El Cubillo pass in the Montes Universales.   This scenery is wonderful, with pine trees lining the narrow road and the sharp grey mountain crests in the distance.

By descending the other side of the pass, you come to a large monument on your left.   This area is where the important Tagus river begins its long journey to the Atlantic through Toledo and Lisbon in Portugal.   It is amazing to see that this important river's origin is a tiny spring flowing out from under a pile of rocks. Continue winding amidst marvelous scenery with expansive views of the valley below until you arrive at the little town of ROYUELO where you bear left and then turn right on TE903 for the 7 kilometer drive to the spectacularly situated little mountain town of ALBARRACIN.   Designated a historical monument by the national government, this whimsical town looks as if it were carved into the living rock below the ruined castle whose towers reach toward the sky.   The Hotel Albarracín's restaurant offers good regional dishes.

Albarracín is a medieval gem with narrow, twisting cobblestoned streets (almost exclusively pedestrian) and ancient brick, stone and wooden houses whose roofs practically touch each other over the tiniest alleyways.   The atmosphere can not have changed much over the past several hundred years.   The handsome cathedral, with its collection of 16th century Brussels tapestries, is interesting to visit, and it is fun to explore the numerous ceramics shops in the village selling their locally made wares.   Since you are only a 30 minute drive from the next destination, you should have leisure time to explore this little Aragonese town; if time is short, do not fail to make the excursion from TERUEL.

A short distance south of Albarracín are some Paleolithic caves with prehistoric paintings. You can get near only one of them by car and to visit the others requires considerable walking, a visit which might best be done as a sidetrip from Teruel, since it will take half a day. Follow the signs leading to the "Pinturas Rupestres". (You see signs as you approach for Cueva del Navazo). A little rock-climbing brings you to the shallow caves protected by an iron grating. Inside are paintings of hunters and bulls. The other caves are farther along the same increasingly impassable road but we do not recommend you attempt to proceed by car.

A pretty easterly drive takes you to Teruel, surrounded by the gorges of the Río Turia. (Soon after leaving Albarracín, glance up to your left for the dramatic sight of ancient castle ruins crowning a rocky vantage point.) Your hotel, the PARADOR NACIONAL DE TERUEL, is located on the left just before you enter Teruel. Recently remodeled, the parador is restful and comfortable, providing the best accommodations available from which to base your explorations of this region, rich in history and archaeology, and of Teruel, rich in Mudéjar monuments.

Besides its remarkable natural setting, Teruel is noteworthy for the dominance of its Mudéjar architecture. Mudéjar is the style created by the Moors who continued to live in Christian-dominated areas after they were reconquered. The Moors remained in Teruel a particularly long time, hence the prevalence of the style here.

The five Mudéjar towers spread around town are of special interest: they are detached belfries with obviously oriental ornamentation. Two of the delicate structures grace the entrance to the old town.

The 13th century cathedral has a fabulous artesonado ceiling of intricately carved wood, with numerous other Mudéjar motifs in the sculptured plaster and in the domed ceilings. The tile decoration is of the same style. One of the five towers serves as the belfry for the cathedral.

P.N. de Teruel
Teruel

Next to St. Peter's church (which has another of the towers as a belfry) is the funerary chapel of the "Lovers of Teruel". The legend of Isabel and Juan Diego, who lived in the 13th century and who died of grief at being unable to marry because of her father's disapproval, has inspired numerous famous literary works, the best-known by the 19th century romantic dramatist Hartzenbusch (thus the name of the street). They were buried in a single grave and their remains are on display here in a glass coffin topped by a recent alabaster relief of the lovers reaching out to touch hands. To visit the chapel, ring at a nearby door (indicated by a sign) and someone will come down to open it for you. (Tip a couple of hundred pesetas.)

Just east is the triangular Plaza del Torico (baby bull), a popular gathering place with a tiny statue of, logically enough, a baby bull in the center.

When you are ready to move on travel north on what must be one of Spain's best country roads towards the tidy farming center of MONREAL DEL CAMPO, at the foot of the Sierra Menera, and bear left by the impressive, tiny fortified town of POZUEL DEL CAMPO with its crumbling walls and huge, imposing church. Continue to MOLINA DE ARAGON, an ancient, pre-Moorish village, once a hotly disputed strongpoint between warring Aragón and Castile.   Perched above the town is a dramatic, red-tinged fortress surrounded by extensive crumbling walls and several restored towers, one of which, the 11th century Torre de Aragón, is a national monument.   This fortress was one of several, including SIGUENZA and ALARCON, which served as a second line of Christian defense during the Reconquest.

Turn north in Monreal del Campo, first along a flat road through farmland, then on a more scenic drive through rugged countryside toward NUEVALOS, a little south of which, in PIEDRA, you will encounter your hotel; just across the Piedra river. Remember the size of this river as you cross it because it will amaze you when you see what it does in the nature park ahead.   Your first view of the monastery will be of the lengthy, sturdy old walls around the grounds, which you follow to the entrance.   The 12th century Cistercian MONASTERIO DE PIEDRA is situated, thanks to the River Piedra, in a green oasis surrounded by red, arid countryside. Your room will be a former monk's cell, but a 12th century monk would hardly recognize it.   Most rooms have a sunny balcony with views of the wooded countryside.

Besides the hotel part of the monastery, there are other interesting remains attached to it and on the surrounding grounds.   The 12th century keep (Torre del Homenaje) is an excellent example of Romanesque-Byzantine style construction. Off the beautiful cloister is a fascinating old kitchen and, next to it, the large monastery dining hall. On the other side of the cloister is the old church, which has not been restored.

The HOTEL MONASTERIO DE PIEDRA is situated next to the principal sight of the area: the lush park watered by the river, which flows through the grounds in capricious ways, forming waterfalls and pools of great beauty. Be sure to visit the series of waterfalls: La Caprichosa (the whimsical lady) and the 170-foot Cola de Caballo (horse's tail), which you can see both from a vistapoint and from underneath in the Iris Grotto. In contrast to the rushing cascades, the lake properly carries the name of Mirror Lake, a truly spectacular natural sight. Buy a ticket at the entrance and follow the arrows for an unforgettable stroll.

Hotel Monasterio de Piedra
Nuévalos

While at the monastery, drive to the pretty little town of NUEVALOS, sitting in a valley surrounded by the deep red hills. Another worthwhile side trip for scenery lovers is to the spa of JARABA, reached by going south to the tiny village of CAMPILLO DE ARAGON and turning right on Z452. You have a 12-kilometer drive through a red, green and gold patchwork quilt of fields as you go over the

Campillo pass. Then you descend into steep canyons lined with dark red cliffs.
This is a dramatic excursion.

DESTINATION IV   ALCAÑIZ   P.N. de la Concordia

Leave this gorgeous setting by heading northeast to CALATAYUD. Today you
will be driving through alternately dusty gray plateaus and deep red earth planted
with fruit trees, vines and olives, along with occasional hay and wheat fields.
Calatayud is built up against a hillside, crowned by the minaret of an old mosque
and the ruins of the Moorish Kalat-Ayub (Castle of Ayub). You might want to
stop for a closer inspection of the Mudéjar tower sitting impressively atop its rocky
ridge above the hillside covered with tiny houses. You can see the castle on the
mountain well before you reach the town, but it blends in so well with the stone
ridge that you may not notice unless you are watching for it.

From here drive southeast, passing the dramatic ruins of a castle near the little
village of MALUENDA, then drive through VELILLA, FUENTES DE JILOCA
and MONTON, all picturesque towns on hilltops overlooking the lush Jiloca river
valley. As you leave Montón notice that vines are beginning to replace fruit trees
on the red landscape.

Turn right on N330 to reach the town of DAROCA. This beautifully situated
medieval town is still enclosed by crumbling 13th century walls with one hundred
and fourteen towers. Park near the first gate you come to and take time to stroll
along the Calle Mayor and visit St. Mary's church and the Plaza Mayor.

Back on N330, drive northeast over the winding Puerto de Paniza pass. As you
descend from the pass you come to CARIÑENA, a little walled town famous for its
wine. If you want to sample or buy some Cariñena wines, the Don Mendo wine

bodega - just near the junction of the C221 and the N330 - makes a convenient stop.

Head east on the C221 driving through seemingly endless vineyards on the undulating reddish-brown hills. A short drive brings you to FUENDETODOS, the birthplace of Francisco de Goya y Lucientes, one of Spain's greatest artists. It is definitely worth a short stop to see the simple house where he lived. The house is furnished with 18th century pieces in an effort to re-create the way it must have looked when Goya lived there. You can even see the room where he was born. Signs direct you to Goya's house and there is no admission charge but a donation (perhaps 100 pesetas per person) is appropriate.

Continue east, through scrubby hills occasionally alternating with lush, green vineyards, to BELCHITE, which was extensively destroyed during the Civil War (1936-39). The rebuilt town stands next to the ruins of the former one as a grim monument to the horror of that conflict. The old town soon appears on the right as you leave: an eerie moonscape of bombed-out buildings, houses and church.

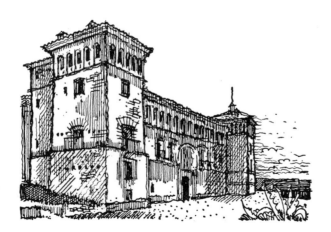

P.N. de la Concordia
Alcañiz

Treasures Off the Beaten Track

A short drive further, after a stretch of fairly flat pasture land lies AZAILA, where you turn south on N232 to HIJAR, another beautiful, small hilltop town overlooking the Martin river from behind its ruined walls. The terrain around the town changes to reflect the ravines carved by the river. From Híjar it is a short drive across flat farmland to ALCAÑIZ.

As you enter town, you see the impressive cathedral ahead and, above on the right, dominating the town, your hotel, the PARADOR NACIONAL DE LA CONCORDIA, itself a national historic monument. Part of the 12th century castle was converted to a palace in the 18th century, and that part now houses the parador. Behind the palace remain some of the original castle buildings, dating from the 12th and 13th centuries. The tower, chapel and cloister can also be visited.

Alcañiz is a delightful little town in the middle of an olive and almond-growing region. The Plaza Mayor is flanked by the town hall with a Renaissance facade, the arcaded 15th century Lonja (trade hall) and the highly elaborate Baroque façade of the colossal St. Mary's collegiate church. Due to its relative isolation, the town has maintained a serene, medieval atmosphere.

DESTINATION V   BARCELONA   Hotel Gran Vía

=====

Head southeast on N420 and N232 and take N420 east towards TARRAGONA where the roads separate. As you leave Alcañiz you see the olive trees slowly give way to vines on the rolling hillsides. About 8 kilometers past CALACEITE, at CASERES, you officially enter Catalonia. Since Catalonians speak (in addition to Spanish) their own language, Catalan, you will find a number of words spelled differently from the way you may be used to (e.g., river is *riu* instead of *río*).

Hotel Gran Vía
Barcelona

GANDESA, rebuilt since it suffered severe destruction during the Civil War and thus a relatively modern town, is at the end of a pretty drive.   After crossing one of Spain's most important rivers, the Ebro, at MORA DE EBRO, the drive arrives at the new town, from where the best view of the old quarter, built right up to the river's edge on the opposite bank, is presented. Now the grape dominates completely as you enter the rich wine-growing valley around FALSET.   The vast vine-clad hills are dotted with tiny villages which seem to float above the vineyards on their little hillocks.   Look back as you leave Falset, for there is an enchanting view of the town.

The highway follows a winding downward course through a number of passes to REUS, the birthplace of architect Antonio Gaudí and known for its wool weaving. The town is now mostly industrial and not particularly appealing to tourists.   Just past Reus join the A2 freeway for a short drive into BARCELONA. You will find the HOTEL GRAN VIA, a charmingly antique-laden inn only steps away from the center of town.

The following itinerary outlines things to do and see during your stay in this attractive city by the Mediterranean Sea.

154

Barcelona Highlights

Barcelona is Spain's second-largest city, but its distinct history and regional culture make it anything but a small-scale Madrid. Its personality, architecture, customs, proximity to France and longterm importance as a Mediterranean seaport make it a sophisticated and cosmopolitan city. The whole region of Catalonia, but especially its capital city of Barcelona, has long resisted absorption by Castile-dominated central authority. Catalans pride themselves on their industriousness and prosperity, both immediately evident to the visitor. Barcelona is a fascinating, bustling, charming city which will enchant you. There is a lot to see and do, so try to budget sufficient time to explore fully the delights the city has to offer.

Plaza Ramón Berenguer

Barcelona Highlights

As in most large, unfamiliar cities, a good way to start your visit is by taking advantage of an organized bus tour, which orients you and gives you a more enlightened idea of how and where to concentrate your time. There are a variety of tours available in English. Ask the hotel concierge to arrange one for you.

Street signs (and maps) are often in the Catalan language. In Barcelona, you will see *carrer* instead of *calle* for street, *passeig* instead of *paseo* for passage, *avinguda* instead of *avenida* for avenue and *placa* instead of *plaza* for town square. The nerve center of the city is the large Plaza de Catalonia on the border between the old city and the new. It is singularly impressive, with many fine monuments and sculptures. Beneath it is the hub of the subway system and the shopping arcades along the underground Avenida de las Luces (Lights).

All of the downtown sights are within walking distance of the plaza, including the festive Ramblas - a cosmopolitan stone-paved promenade running generally south from the plaza to the waterfront. Ramblas comes from the Arabic for river bed, which is what this once was. Now it is a chic and shady street, lined with shops and hotels and frequented by anyone and everyone visiting Barcelona. At the plaza end are kiosks selling newspapers and books in many languages, then a bird market takes over and the street is adorned with cages full of colorful birds. Next are lovely flower stalls, then a series of tree-shaded cafes, perfect for people watching. On the right side of the street (as you walk toward the waterfront), just before you reach the flower stalls you find a busy public market which is fun to stroll through to see the amazing variety of produce and fresh fish that Barcelonans have to choose from.

At the waterfront end of Ramblas is a monument to Columbus and a re-creation of his famous ship, the Santa María. King Ferdinand and Queen Isabella were holding court here when he returned from his first voyage and he gave them the news of his discovery of a route to the Orient (he still thought this is what he had found). Visit the Santa María and try to imagine what it would be like to set out into unknown waters on a two-month voyage as Columbus did in this tiny ship in

1492. You can also take boat rides around the harbor from here.

A few blocks east of the Ramblas is the colorful Gothic Quarter (Barrio Gótico), a maze of old buildings, streets and alleyways. A marvelous 15th century cathedral dominates the area, which also contains the city hall (ayuntamiento), with its lovely sculptures and paintings and beautifully decorated chambers and halls. There are lots of atmospheric *"tapa"* bars and chic shops, including some interesting antique stores, in this lively area.

Still farther east is the famed Calle Montcada, lined with handsome old mansions. Two of these contain the Picasso Museum with an impressive display of virtually every period of the famous painter's work. Although born in Málaga, Picasso spent much of his life (especially during his formative years) in Barcelona. His most famous paintings are not here, but the museum contains many examples of his early work.

The Holy Family Church
Barcelona

Even more intriguing are the works of another famous Barcelona artist, Antonio Gaudí (1852-1926), the avant-garde architect. The Holy Family (Sagrada Familia) Church is the city's most famous landmark, its perforated spires visible from various points around the city. Best reached by cab, you certainly want to take a closer look at the marvelous unfinished building with its intricately carved facades and molten-rock textures. Even more fanciful is the Guell Park overlooking the city (Eusebio Guell was a wealthy patron of Gaudí); also unfinished, but delightful in its conception and whimsical atmosphere. (Many of Gaudí's imaginative creations resemble lifesize gingerbread houses.) Numerous examples of his work can be found in the city: the Casa Batlló, Casa Mila, and the Pedrera are on the Paseo de Gracia, west of the Plaza de Catalunya, and the Palacio Guell is just off the Ramblas. They all attest to the apparent rejection of the straight line as a design element in the highly individualistic style of this innovative artist. Because they cannot be moved from Barcelona, they are more an integral part of the city's personality than the paintings of Picasso or Miró which can be seen in art museums all over the world.

Another not-to-be-missed area is the Parque de Montjuich, occupying the hill of the same name south of the Plaza de Catalunya. Originally the site of a defensive fort built in the 17th century (which now contains a military museum), a number of interesting public buildings were erected here for the 1929 exposition. (This is a branch of the same exposition for which a number of buildings in the Parque de Maria Luisa were constructed in Seville. The exposition was divided between the two cities.) The Museum of Catalan Art is in the Palacio Nacional and it contains fine Gothic and Romanesque sections, featuring wonderful examples of religious art that have been rescued from abandoned churches all over the region. These are magnificently displayed, often as complete church interiors.

Also in Montjuich is the Pueblo Español (Spanish town) which is an entire little village, constructed for the 1929 exposition, utilizing the varied architectural styles of Spain. Some of the structures are re-creations of actual buildings, and some simply imitate regional styles. The entrance, for example, is a reconstruction of the towers of the city wall of Avila. It is an impressive achievement and is now essentially a shopping area featuring *artesanía* (arts and crafts) from the different regions. If you have been to other areas of Spain, you will be struck by the unique juxtaposition of the various architectural styles.

Montjuich is also the setting of one of the most wonderful of all the sights in Barcelona - the beautiful dancing fountains (*fuentes*). For a truly unforgetable experience, ask at your hotel for the times they are augmented with lights and music (it was Thursday, Saturday and Sunday from 10:00PM to 11:00PM when we were there, but such schedules are subject to change). Music from classical to contemporary accompanies the multi-colored, ever-changing spouts in a symphony of sensory experience. If you go an hour early and are prepared to wile away the time watching the Barcelonans stroll around the park, you will also be able to secure a seat in front of the palace.

Also in the park is the Fundación Joan Miró, with several hundred examples of this native son's bold and colorful paintings, along with works by other contemporary artists - definitely worth a visit if you are a modern art devotee.

Barcelona has long been known for the quality and variety of its restaurants. We especially like the Hotel Ritz dining room, which is convenient if you are downtown at lunchtime. A short cab ride away is the quietly elegant and excellent Restaurante Reno (at Tuset, 27) with a sophisticated atmosphere on a fairly quiet street. The menu is international and the prices are what you would expect to find in a deluxe restaurant. For a less formal atmosphere, try the Hostal Sant Jordi (Travessera de Dalt, 123), also a short cab ride from downtown. Their menu features regional Catalan cuisine at reasonable prices. Barcelona is one of the few places in Spain where restaurants tend to close early (10:00 PM). If you find yourself wanting to eat later, the Restaurante Lluria, across the side street from the Ritz, is open until midnight and also serves local specialties at modest prices.

There is ample nightlife in Barcelona. The best approach is to ask your hotel concierge, since shows change constantly. One permanent offering, however, is the Scala, an international, Las Vegas-style review which is very professionally presented and is enjoyable even if you do not have an understanding of the Spanish language. There is a dinner show - the food is only passable - and a later show at midnight without dinner. You need to ask your hotel concierge to make reservations for the Scala, since it is highly popular both with locals and tourists.

Children will particularly enjoy the new amusement park on the Montjuich hill, and an older one, reached by funicular railway, on the hill called Tibidabo. Both spots have fine city views. In the Parque de la Ciudadela there is a good zoo.

The Costa Brava
and Beyond

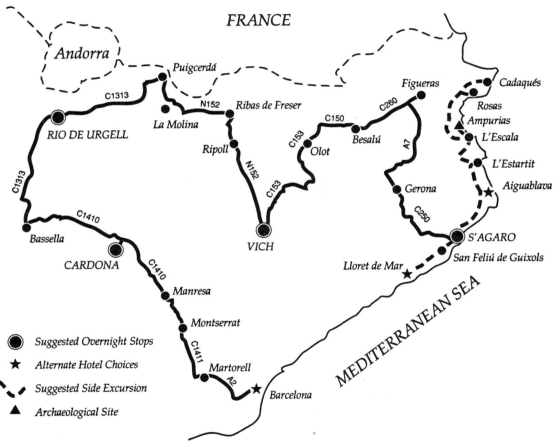

FRANCE

Andorra

Puigcerdá

C1313

RIO DE URGELL

La Molina

N152

Ribas de Freser

Ripoll

N152

C153

C150

Olot

Besalú

C260

Figueras

Cadaqués

Rosas

Ampurias

L'Escala

L'Estartit

Aiguablava

C1313

Bassella

C1410

CARDONA

C1410

Manresa

Montserrat

C1411

Martorell

A2

VICH

Gerona

A7

C250

S'AGARO

San Feliú de Guixols

Lloret de Mar

Barcelona

MEDITERRANEAN SEA

Suggested Overnight Stops

★ Alternate Hotel Choices

Suggested Side Excursion

▲ Archaeological Site

161

The Costa Brava and Beyond

This itinerary is essentially a tour of Catalonia, and it includes a sampling of the multiple delights to be savored in this region: spectacular mountains, lovely old towns and castles and beautiful sea coasts that alternate cliffs and beaches.

Catalonia has been settled continuously since the Greeks landed in the 6th century B.C. In the 15th century Catalonia combined with Aragon to form a vast kingdom extending to Naples, Italy, and it became, somewhat reluctantly, part of the new kingdom created by the marriage of Ferdinand, King of Aragón, to Isabella, Queen of Castile.

Besalú

Catalonia has fiercely defended its autonomy during its entire history. As a Republican stronghold in the Civil War of 1936-1939, the region experienced a great deal of the bloodshed. When the Nationalists (under Franciso Franco) won, regional autonomy was suppressed. Only after the adoption of the new constitution of 1978 were the various regions allowed to regain a measure of autonomy, and Catalonia was the first to do so.

In addition to Spanish, the regional language of Catalan is widely used. As in Galicia and the Basque country, you often see things spelled in the regional dialect. Since 1978, most official signs have been replaced with bilingual ones. Cuisine in Catalonia vies with that of the Basque region for the title of best in the country. It includes many seafood and meat dishes with a variety of sauces, reminiscent - and imitative - of French culinary style. In Catalonia, the mixture of sandy beaches, rugged coastlines, gorgeous mountain scenery and fine food offers something for everyone.

ORIGINATING CITY   BARCELONA

Barcelona is an impressive and prosperous city with much to see and do. But the rest of Catalonia also has much to offer, so when you have completed a tour of Barcelona, head into the interior to see another side of this lovely region.

DESTINATION I   CARDONA   P.N. Duques de Cardona

Leave Barcelona by going south on the A2 freeway to exit 25 just outside of town. Turn right on NII to MARTORELL, an ancient town where the Llobregat river is spanned by the Puente (bridge) del Diablo, said to have been built by the Carthaginian general Hannibal in 218 B.C. He erected the triumphal arch in honor of his father Hamilcar Barca. Continue on NII to ABRERA and bear right on C1411 to reach MONTSERRAT, whose ragged, stark grey silhouette makes you see instantly why it is called "serrated mountain". After entering the village of MONISTROL, follow the signs to the monastery on top of the hill - about 7 kilometers, along a zigzagging road offering ever-more-magnificent views. You could opt for the cable car (funicular) from a clearly marked point just before Monistrol, if you would rather avoid the mountain driving and the sometimes severe parking problem up top. Taking the cable car certainly makes the trip more enjoyable for the driver.

The golden-brown monastery at the crown of Montserrat contrasts strikingly with the jutting grey peaks of the mountain. The setting is ultra-dramatic, and it is claimed that on a clear day you can see the Balearic Islands in the Mediterranean. The monastery church is home to the famed Moreneta, or Black Madonna. The figure, reportedly made by St. Luke, and brought to Barcelona by St. Peter, was hidden in the Santa Cueva (holy cave) at the time of the Moorish invasions, then found by shepherds in the 9th century. This is the patron saint of Catalonia, and is venerated by thousands of pilgrims annually. Numerous marked paths and cable cars will take you to various viewpoints as well as the monastery along the 22 kilometer massif.

After you have visited this marvelous mountain, one of the most famous in the world for its unusual appearance and the inspiration for Montsalvat in Wagner's "Parsifal", return to Monistrol and turn left to MANRESA. Visit the elaborate 14th century collegiate church of Santa Maria de la Seo on a rocky cliff above the town. Follow the signs for SOLSONA and, as you leave town, do not fail to look back to catch a spectacular view of Montserrat in the distance. Follow the Rio Cardoner through red, pine-covered ridges, punctuated with little farming towns, to CARDONA, beautifully situated, and crowned by an outstanding fortress/castle, which just happens to be your hotel, the PARADOR NACIONAL DUQUES DE

CARDONA. This magnificent parador retains much of its 10th and 11th century construction, and the purely Romanesque Collegiate Church of St. Vincent is in the center.

P.N. Duques de Cardona
Cardona

Cardona's earliest significance was as a source of salt for the Romans. The conical mountain of salt to the south of town has been mined for centuries. The town itself is very quiet unless you happen to be there on Sunday, which is market day, when things are considerably busier. And, if you time your visit for the first half of September, you can experience the annual festival with a "running of the bulls", similar to that of Pamplona.

A lovely side trip is to the ancient brown and red village of SOLSONA, about 15 minutes away, which is entered through a stone gate in the old town wall. It has a salt and craft museum, and a quaint old quarter for wandering. The parador in Cardona is wonderful, but Solsona is a more interesting town than Cardona.

Head northwest out of Cardona following a lovely stretch of road through rugged hillsides, dotted with ruins of castles and monasteries, through SOLSONA (worth a stop if you did not make the side trip above).

Continue to BASELLA, then turn north, following the Segre river for the 50 kilometer drive to LA SEO DE URGEL. At this point, the Pyrenees begin to make their brooding presence known in the distance ahead. Travel across the Segre river to reach the beautiful aquamarine Oliana reservoir. From the banks of the reservoir are splendid views of the lake surrounded by its grey-green sheer cliffs, which occasionally seem almost man-made - like giant stone edifices. At the other end of the reservoir is COLL DE NARGO, then ORGANYA, both tiny villages stacked on the hillside like layer cakes. Beyond Organya, the cliffs become steeper and closer as you traverse the deep Organya gorge.   The grey cliffs rise to 2,000 feet here and make an impressive backdrop before you come out into the fertile valley where Seo De Urgel (named for its episcopal see, founded in 820) is located.   The town's unique, modern parador, the PARADOR NACIONAL DE LA SEO DE URGEL, is an unexpected and pleasurable surprise. Constructed on the 14th century site of a church and convent, the decor in the public rooms is enhanced by the stone arches that remain from the original cloister. The prevailing theme of the decor is contemporary, but tasteful and spacious.

You will enjoy strolling the old quarter around the parador. After working up an appetite, an excellent place for dining is the Castellciutat Motel. It is located near the castle remains just south of town and is a very popular dining spot, so it is advisable to have a reservation for a table with a valley view (the parador staff will be glad to make it for you).

A suggested excursion includes travel from Spain to ANDORRA, across into

France and then back again to Spain, all in the course of a day. Just 9 kilometers north of Seo you reach the border of the tiny principality of Andorra, which is under the joint administration of the Bishop of Urgel and the French government. (Although border formalities are usually perfunctory, you will need your passport and your green card showing proof of auto insurance.)

P.N. de la Seo de Urgel
Seo de Urgel

Recognized throughout history for the fierce independence of its residents, Andorra is now known mostly as a duty-free zone, and thus a shopper's paradise. You see an infinite number of stores selling imported goods lining the streets of the capital, ANDORRA LA VELLA. Besides shopping, Andorra offers mountain scenery *sans pareil*. You ascend through pine forests crowned by the barren, blue-grey, snow-dotted peaks of the Pyrenees. It is truly a breathtaking drive. You will see numerous ski areas as you cross the Envalira Pass and descend the mountainside to the French border. From here it is a short drive through the French Pyrenees to the quaint little town of BOURG MADAME, where a fine meal can be enjoyed at the Hostal Cerdane. Just outside of town you cross back into Spain at PUIGCERDA, a small fortified border town. From here head west through the pretty valley of the Segre river back to Seo.

NOTE: If time precludes this as a side trip, it can be included in the next destination route, but this will not allow any time for shopping in Andorra and it makes for a long day's drive through a lot of mountain passes.

DESTINATION III   VICH   P.N. de Vich

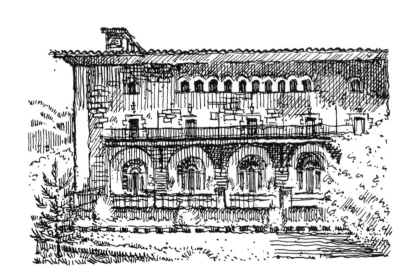

P.N. de Vich
Vich

When you are ready to move on, more beautiful mountain vistas await. Leaving Seo head east to PUIGCERDA tracing the Segre river. Follow the signs for PUERTO DE TOSES and BARCELONA and head south on N152 along a mountainside with terrific views of the deep valley below. Soon you will spot the ski resort of LA MOLINA in the green valley below.

The road winds through green mountains as you approach RIBAS DE FRESER, a charming little village of pastel-colored buildings. In a short while, if you keep an eye out to your right, you will see a waterfall bursting from the hillside. It is not far to RIPOLL, a pretty town with pitched red-tile roofs topping tall, narrow buildings on the Ter river, and the home of a 9th century Benedictine monastery founded by Visigothic Count Wilfred "the Hairy". Wilfred was responsible for freeing Catalonia from the domination of Charlemagne. The Ripoll library was once one of the largest in the Christian world.

As you approach the ancient town of VICH, watch for a castle on the hill to the right. Your hotel is out of town. You see signs in Vich directing you to it. The PARADOR NACIONAL DE VICH is a new parador built in the regional *"masia catalana"* style to resemble an old Catalonian manor house. The visual effect as you approach is stunning, with a view of the dramatic red and white stone cliffs surrounding the blue reservoir.

At some point during your stay here go into the town of Vich and visit the pretty Plaza Mayor, surrounded by the 15th century town hall and a 16th century palace. A short distance down the Calle de Riera is the neoclassical cathedral.

DESTINATION IV   S'AGARO   Hostal de la Gavina
══

It is hard to leave the Parador Nacional's marvelous location, but it will help to know that your next stop is equally wonderful in an entirely different way. Return to the C153 and turn right to begin the next stretch of your journey. A short drive brings you to the turnoff to the exquisitely preserved, 16th century town of RUPIT, which you reach past a huge grey mesa, itself a dramatic sight. Rupit is an utterly charming, typical northern-Spanish town. Park outside the gate and stroll through the age-old cobblestone streets and plazas with their stone houses and iron balconies hung with colorful flowers. It is a perfect place for pictures and old-world atmosphere pervades. There is a restaurant on your left just before you enter town where you can stop for coffee.

The drive from Vich to the medieval town of OLOT is particularly lovely. The variety of scenery is incredible - vast forests crowned by rugged grey cliffs and mesas give way to equally beautiful vast fertile plains with the blue Pyrenees as a backdrop. The spectacular scenery and poor road surface dictate a leisurely pace.

Just beyond Olot, where the road improves considerably, you drive through CASTELLFOLLIT DE LA ROCA which, on your approach, appears ordinary. Be sure, however, to stop and look back at it from the other side, where you will realize that it is built on a giant rock at the very edge of a deep ravine - a spectacular photo opportunity.

Your next stop, BESALU, requires similar treatment. Go through town, cross the bridge, then turn around and come back for a spellbinding view of this perfectly preserved medieval town. Stop for a while in this town because the lovely little Plaza de la Libertad is wonderfully typical of ancient Spanish towns. It is an atmospheric and picturesque place to sit for a while and watch the activity in the colorful square.

Leaving Besalú follow signs to FIGUERAS. Fully hope that the hour is approaching lunchtime, because, just before town, you see a sign for the Mas Pau restaurant, one of Spain's finest (worth planning your day around). In an ivy-covered, old stone farmhouse, the restaurant features numerous quaint dining rooms and, best of all, a lovely terrace overlooking the flowering patio and the surrounding farmland. Meals are exquisite and you will linger over every morsel of your elegantly served and presented meal. You might start off with a variation on the *gazpacho* theme called *Cap de Creus*, which adds shrimp and clams to the basic recipe; followed by salmon and caviar in a puff pastry, and a sole and lobster duet. Their special dessert is simply a sampling of everything on the cart - unbelievable, but a challenge to be met like a trooper.

A 5-kilometer drive brings you to Figueras, the birthplace of surrealistic painter Salvador Dali (1904-1989). If surrealism interests you, we positively recommend a visit to the bizarre Teatro Museo Dali where numerous (often humorous) paintings and sculptures by the famous artist are displayed.

Hostal de la Gavina
S'Agaró

You will be glad to find there is a freeway connecting Figueras to GERONA and a good highway from there to S'AGARO (take the Gerona South exit to SAN FELIU DE GUIXOLS and then the coast road a couple of kilometers north.) The HOSTAL DE LA GAVINA (seagull), the next destination, is one of Spain's premier hotels, just north of the little town. Settle in for a few days of luxurious relaxation overlooking the beautiful Costa Brava.

S'Agaró is a small beach town sandwiched between two larger, more lively resorts - San Feliu and PLATJA D'ARO. Both are worth a visit for their chic shops, huge white sand beaches and animated cafes and restaurants.

If you are in the mood for an excursion from your lovely hotel, return to Figueras on the freeway and head northeast toward LLANSA. You pass through rather barren country at first and, before you reach Llansa, you see the CASTELLO DE QUERMANCO on your right. Watch carefully, because it almost blends into the landscape on the hillside. From Llansa turn south down the Costa Brava (Wild Coast) - a lot less brava than it used to be with the appearance every few miles of another little resort settlement filled with white cottages with red-tile roofs and all the support and entertainment services that go with them. But the sea and the rugged coastline are as beautiful as ever. The water is a clear, deep blue and dotted with sail- and fishing boats. Continue south through EL PUERTO DE LA SELVA, then wind the scenic way to CADAQUES, a whitewashed and picturesque fishing-town-cum-artist-colony that surrounds the harbor. Take time to stroll along the waterfront and enjoy the play of the light on the colorful fishing boats. If your visit coincides with mealtime, consider the Don Quijote restaurant with its ivy-covered terrace. The food is delicious and the restaurant deservedly rates a Michelin star.

Retrace your steps 5 kilometers and take a left toward ROSAS, located on a bay of the same name. Once a typical fishing village, Rosas (and most "villages" along this coast) is fast becoming a holiday resort. Continue to the walled, old market town of CASTELLO DE AMPURIAS, turn south across the fruit-tree-dotted Ampurdán plain, turn left near VILADAMAT and follow the signs leading to the archaeological excavation at AMPURIAS. Scipio landed here in the Second Punic War in 219 B.C. The town was founded in the 6th century B.C. as a Greek trading station. Tour the Neapolis, with many ancient walls and original floors. A museum displays the interesting artifacts that have been uncovered.

A short freeway journey returns you to S'Agaró and the Hostal de la Gavina.

Other nearby spots to visit are reached by heading up the coast to Platja d'Aro, PALAMOS, and CALELLA, a pretty resort town with an impressive botanical garden on a cliff overlooking the sea at CAP ROIG, just to the south of town. The beautifully planned and located garden has a shady walk through flowers and trees and spectacular views over the sea.

If you go south through San Feliu and continue along the coast toward TOSSA DE MAR and LLORET DE MAR, you have a breathtaking and dramatic drive along a winding corniche road carved into the mountainside above the deep blue sea. The rugged cliffs demonstrate clearly why this is called the wild coast. Tossa de Mar is a pretty little beach town with a harbor, and your first sight of it - crowned by a castle and surrounded by 12th century walls and impressive round towers - is magnificent. Lloret de Mar has a long golden beach, which makes it exceedingly popular during the summer months (when its population more than triples). The Hotel Roger de Flor, in an old manor home on a hill above town, has a charming terrace patio, and makes a lovely spot for lunch.

Tossa de Mar

The Costa Brava and Beyond

Spain

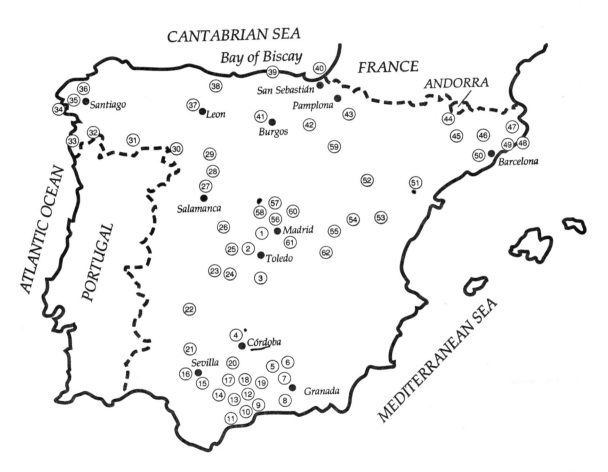

CANTABRIAN SEA

Bay of Biscay

FRANCE

ANDORRA

ATLANTIC OCEAN

PORTUGAL

MEDITERRANEAN SEA

Santiago

Leon

San Sebastián

Pamplona

Burgos

Salamanca

Madrid

Toledo

Barcelona

Córdoba

Sevilla

Granada

175

On a promontory overlooking an incredibly blue inlet on the Costa Brava, dotted with boats and rocky beaches, is a real gem of a hotel, the Aigua Blava. You feel at home from the moment you enter this superbly managed, recently remodeled establishment. Its gregarious multilingual proprietor, nicknamed "Xiquet", whose family converted their home into a small hotel in 1940 after it was returned to them following the disastrous civil war, is ever present and will extend a personal greeting during the course of your stay. Now a fairly large hotel, the Aigua Blava retains the atmosphere of several homes, jumbled together around flowered terraces and *"rinconcitos"* (little corners). Decorated by family members, each room is unique - from simple to elaborate - and many have sea views and terraces (for a surcharge). Set under a slanted ceiling, the "Chez Xiquet" room contains family memorabilia, looks out to a large terrace and a fantastic view. For any room, however, reservations should be made well in advance during high season, as many guests return here year after year for their week or two in the sun. For a relaxing sojourn in an enchanting seaside spot with family atmosphere, you can't go wrong at the Aigua Blava.

HOTEL AIGUA BLAVA
Playa de Fornells
17255 Aiguablava, Gerona
tel: (72)622058 telex: 57077
76 rooms - Pts 7,000
Open: March 29 to October 21
Credit cards: all major
Restaurant, pool, tennis
U.S. Rep: NIC Tours
Rep tel: (415) 871-6680
Nearest airport: Barcelona (116 km)
Nearest train station: Flassa (28 km)

On the high, isolated, tree-covered point of Esmuts, overlooking the open sea on one side and a turquoise bay on the other, is the P.N. de la Costa Brava - a modern, secluded hideaway for the visitor seeking every comfort on the Wild Coast. Unlike most paradors, this one does not strive for an antique ambiance. The attractive public rooms are airy and open, accented in bright spring colors, and the bedrooms are spacious and bright with red-tiled floors and terraces with lovely views of either the ocean or the bay.   There are six extra-large special rooms (*habitaciones especiales*), with large round bathtubs, separate, sunken showers and exercise areas featuring exercycles and weights. For our money, these are "special" enough to merit surprisingly few additional pesetas.   There is however, in addition, a public exercise/game room downstairs with saunas.   The guest here is two minutes by a footpath from the beach on the bay or can save the effort and choose to lounge around the lovely fresh-water pool overlooking the ocean.   For a short or long stay, this contemporary parador above the idyllic, white town of Aiguablava is an excellent choice.

P.N. DE LA COSTA BRAVA
17255 Aiguablava, Gerona
tel: (72)622162 telex: 56275
fax: 622166
87 rooms - Pts 11,000
Credit cards: all major
Restaurant, pool
U.S. Rep: NIC Tours
Rep tel: (415) 871-6680
Nearest airport: Barcelona (116 km)
Nearest train station: Flassa (28 km)

This spectacular parador crowns the tiny fortified town of Alarcón on the rocky central meseta south of Madrid. Perched on a promontory, this dramatic 8th-century Arab fortress resembles an island surrounded by the deep, natural gorges created by the looping Júcar river below. The imposing castle-hotel is superbly preserved and retains a considerable portion of its original construction, including crenellated towers, ramparts and the vigilant castle keep, featuring a guestroom on each floor. The main lounge off the entry patio is awe-inspiring: its towering, stone and wood-beamed ceiling arches over gigantic tapestries, suits of armor and a corner fireplace - you can all but hear the rattling of swords borne by the Knights of the Order of St. James who readied themselves here to combat the Moors during the Reconquest. There are few guestrooms, and each is unique, though they all feature traditional Castilian wood furnishings, high ceilings, breathtaking views beyond thick walls, and a minibar. Room 3 has windows so high that steps are carved to reach them, and room 1 has an impressive exposed-stone bóveda ceiling. Don't fail to take a turn around the ramparts during your stay here - it will make you realize why the Moors chose it as a stronghold and wonder how the Christians ever wrested it from them.

P.N. MARQUES DE VILLENA
Avenida Amigos del Castillo, s/n
16213 Alarcón, Cuenca
tel: (66)331350
13 rooms - Pts 10,000
Credit cards: all major
U.S. Rep: NIC Tours
Rep tel: (415) 871-6680
Nearest airport: Valencia (170 km)
Nearest train station: Cuenca (85 km)

Perched on an overhang in one of the most perfectly preserved medieval towns in Spain you will find the Hotel Albarracín, situated in a 16th century palace that was once the home of one of the leading ladies of the region.   Recently acquired by an important Spanish hotel chain, the Albarracín retains some of its past elegance, most notably in the lobby with its heavy wood beams and staircase, in the hallways sprinkled with antiques, and in the restaurant, which serves very good regional specialties at very reasonable prices (the house salad and the migas, fried breadcrumbs with bacon, are particularly noteworthy).   Unfortunately, in the effort to modernize, charm has been largely overlooked in the small, simply furnished bedrooms where linoleum now covers the original stone or wood floors. However, the Albarracín has a pretty little pool, is perfectly located at the edge of the old town (though this does make parking difficult) and is moderately priced, making it the best choice for the traveler who wishes to spend a full day wandering the tiny streets of this ancient town and exploring the archaeologically rich surrounding countryside.

HOTEL ALBARRACIN
Calle Azagra
41100 Albarracín, Teruel
tel: (74)710011
42 rooms - Pts 7,550
Credit cards: all major
Restaurant, pool
Nearest airport: Zaragoza (191 km)
Nearest train station: Teruel (38 km)

The Oromana is within easy driving distance of Seville but wonderfully isolated from the hubbub of the big city. Set in the countryside, surrounded by a cool, green pine grove, the white Oromana resembles an Andalusian villa, with lovely wrought-iron balconies, grillwork and the typical red-tile roof. The public rooms are tastefully furnished and casually inviting. The marble-columned sitting room with its vaulted ceiling is especially nice. The smallish guest rooms are simply furnished but comfortable and all have lovely views of the tranquil natural park on the Guadaira river: it is the setting that really makes this an outstanding choice of hotel. The hotel is air-conditioned throughout, a welcome touch in the heat of the Andalusian summer. The grassy pool area is very appealing and adds greatly to the restful atmosphere of the place. This is the hotel chosen by Spanish soccer teams that come to play Seville, and by NASA personnel when they come to man the nearby space-shuttle tracking station. They are all looking for peace and quiet and the manager, Señor Martínez, strives to provide it. Just a 15-minute drive from Seville, one can avoid city driving altogether by taking a bus that leaves the sleepy little suburban town of Alcalá every half hour for the city.

HOTEL OROMANA
Avenida de Portugal, s/n
41500 Alcalá de Guadaira, Sevilla
tel: (54)700804
30 rooms - Pts 7,000
Credit cards: AX VS MC
Restaurant, pool
Nearest airport: Seville (12 km)
Nearest train station: Seville (12 km)

Dominating the town of Alcañiz and the beautifully fertile Maestrazgo valley, the P.N. de la Concordia is installed in a majestic 18th century Aragonese palace, once a 12th century castle.   Its double rooms have extensive views framed by thick castle walls and wooden windows (some windows set so high that steps have been built in to reach them), lovely rustic wood furnishings, pale-blue bedspreads and burnished red-tile floors highlighted by colorfully patterned rugs.   Due to the spaciousness of the beamed hallways, sitting areas, beautiful, high-ceilinged dining room and handsome lounge the palace has deceptively few rooms to accommodate guests. Your visit here will be a trip back through time.   A 12th century tower that was constructed when the Knights of the Order of Calatrava were based here is found on the grounds, and a small cloister and the remains of walls dating from the 12th through the 15th centuries share the hotel's dramatic hilltop setting.   Medieval Alcañiz and its parador offer a lovely and tranquil stop for the traveler.

P.N. DE LA CONCORDIA
Castillo de Calatravos
44600 Alcañiz, Teruel
tel: (74)830400
12 rooms - Pts 9,000
Open: February through December
Credit cards: all major
Restaurant, medieval building
U.S. Rep: NIC Tours
Rep tel: (415) 871-6680
Nearest airport: Zaragoza (105 km)
Nearest train station: Caspe (8 km)

In the verdant Andalusian hills, ten minutes from Mijas and less than an hour from the bustle of Malaga and the beaches of the Costa del Sol, a 300-year-old farmhouse has been restored with rustic originality and reopened as a country inn by Arun Narang, an American, and his British wife, Jean. The rambling, red-roofed building is surrounded by orchards, grazing horses and a grass-edged swimming pool. The horses are available to the guests for a thousand pesetas an outing, and an interesting, international menu and barbecue are offered on a shady terrace near the pool. Enclosed within whitewashed walls are several garden patios, a charming sitting-room/bar lined with books and enhanced with a cozy fireplace, a billiard room (where the former owner once housed lions), a small interior restaurant and six bedrooms. Only one of the guestrooms has a private bath; two others share one bath, and the remaining three share two. The rooms are on the small side (those upstairs a bit larger), differ in orientation and are decorated simply with appealing, dark-wood furniture and fresh white bedspreads. Breakfast is included with the room, and full board for two costs just 11,000 pesetas. For a budget getaway (but not too far), the Finca provides a unique ambiance and a friendly atmosphere.

FINCA LA MOTA
Lista de Correos
29120 Alhaurín el Grande, Málaga
tel: (52)491112
6 rooms - Pts 5,000
Credit cards: all major
Restaurant, pool, horses
Nearest airport: Málaga (30 km)
Nearest train station: Fuengirola (15 km)

This parador is surprisingly not a bonafide restoration of the 16th century original, but was in fact built in 1979, and principally the entry and attached church are all that remain of the former 1596 convent. However, the newness is hard to detect and you will marvel at the attention to detail. Everything from the bricks to the windows to the rough stones used for the floor were custom made. Elegant antiques abound in the public rooms. Cozy, quiet sitting areas, often with fireplaces, are located on each floor and sixteen lovely patios are spaced invitingly around the premises. The bedrooms are impressive, with ancient-looking windows and quaint wooden beds surrounded by pretty ceramic-tiled walls instead of headboards. The other furnishings are harmonious in style and color, contrasting delightfully with the whitewashed walls. The bar is similarly enchanting: built in the style of an old wine cellar, it holds giant clay vats which extend from the lower sitting area through the floor above. Surrounding the vats are rough wooden tables which complete the ancient bodega atmosphere.

P.N. DE ALMAGRO
Ronda de San Francisco
13270 Almagro, Ciudad Real
tel: (26)860100
55 rooms - Pts 8,500
Credit cards: all major
Restaurant, pool
U.S. Rep: NIC Tours
Rep tel: (415) 871-6680
Nearest airport: Madrid (218 km)
Nearest train station: Ciudad Real (22 km)

This 1980s addition to the parador chain is of modern, whitewashed construction, built on a high point in town and overlooking the green sea of the Antequera plain. Just an hour from Málaga and two from Granada, it offers a restful, rural alternative to city sounds and pace, in a town with no less than 38 churches and 3 remarkable prehistoric dolmens. The dining room and vast lounge are on split levels, complemented with a blonde-wood cathedral ceiling and contemporary furniture. Wall-to wall windows afford expansive countryside views from both. An immaculate green-and-white hallway leads past a tiny, sunlit interior patio to the guestrooms, all identical, with good-size white-tile baths, brick-red floors with beige-weave rugs, pastel-print bedspreads and wood and leather furnishings. All the rooms have lovely views, though if you request "una habitación en la segunda planta con vista de la vega" you'll get the best orientation. If you make a reststop here, don't fail to visit nearby El Torcal, an incredible natural display of rock formations.

P.N. DE ANTEQUERA
Paseo García de Olmo
29200 Antequera, Málaga
tel: (52)840261
fax: 840991
55 rooms - Pts 8,000
Credit cards: all major
Pool
U.S. Rep: NIC Tours
Rep tel: (415) 871-6680
Nearest airport: Málaga (58 km)
Nearest train station: Antequera

This wonderfully situated inn was built in 1966 on the site of an old mansion on the Plaza de Espana in the center of the hilltop white town of Arcos. With the attention to authenticity characteristic of the parador architects, this parador was restored and reopened in 1985 and appears as a mansion several centuries old. The lobby and lounges are accented with antiques and enlivened with ceramic tile pictures. The hallways are elegant with either open-beamed or lovely vaulted ceilings. Off the dining room is an enclosed garden patio that features an old tiled, stone well - a delightful spot for refreshment. The patio faces stiff competition from the terrace off the pretty little bar, which offers an endlessly dramatic view over the vast plains far below. The spacious bedrooms are extremely attractive, appointed with dark, carved-wood beds and deep red drapes and bedspreads which contrast beautifully with the stark white walls. Rooms either overlook the town's picturesque main square, or, for a small surcharge, you can request a room with its own terrace overlooking the valley.

P.N. CASA DEL CORREGIDOR
Plaza de Espana, 5
11630 Arcos de la Frontera, Cadiz
tel: (56)700500
24 rooms - Pts 9,500
Credit cards: all major
Restaurant
U.S. Rep: NIC Tours
Rep tel: (415) 871-6680
Nearest airport: Seville (105 km)
Nearest train station: Jerez (40 km)

From the 14th until the 18th centuries, one of the most influential families in the ancient walled town of Avila lived next to the cathedral in the mansion which is today the Gran Hotel Valderrábanos. Their escutcheons can still be seen above the magnificent stone entryway, which today leads into a marble-floored reception area accented with genuine suits of armor. Antiques are generously distributed throughout the grand, high-ceilinged public rooms. The bedrooms are pleasingly and comfortably furnished with occasional antiques, hand-woven rugs and original art works. They are reached, however, after navigating what must be the darkest hallways in hostelry. Of the three suites, number 229 is most impressive: on two levels, it has vaulted ceilings and a view across the rooftop to the cathedral. Some front doubles also look onto the cathedral square, but they are noisier than the interior rooms. Breakfast is served in the cozy English pub-style bar. The restaurant is quite good (try the gazpacho), although somewhat lacking in ambiance. The hotel is a fine choice in the ancient walled town of Avila, both for its location and creative maintenance of its historic situation.

GRAN HOTEL PALACIO VALDERRABANOS
Plaza de la Catedral, 6
05001 Avila
tel: (18)211023 telex: 23539
73 rooms - Pts 8,400 ~
Credit cards: all major
Restaurant
Nearest airport: Madrid (113 km)
Nearest train station: Avila

Tucked just within the walls of Avila, the first fortified Romanesqu
is the P.N. Raimundo de Borgoña. Partially installed within
home of Piedras Albas, both the renovated palace and the h...
tastefully in keeping with the original architectural style. The massive gi...
limestone and wrought-iron staircase off the lobby testifies to the success of this
intention. The decor is an attractive mix of regional-style furniture and antique
elements. You should stroll in the evening along the city ramparts in the pretty
back gardens to enjoy a panorama of both the town and the surrounding
countryside. The bedrooms are spacious and well-decorated, with tradi|tional
Spanish furnishings, wood floors and views of the town walls, the garden or the
narrow streets of Avila - each equally inviting. The gracefully columned interior
patio's focus is on its stone bull - a traditional symbol of nobility in the ancient
Iberian (pre-historic) past. In the bar are the original Arabic tiles salvaged from
this patio. This parador is for the discriminating guest looking for ambiance and
comfort.

P.N. RAIMUNDO DE BORGOÑA
Marqués de Canales de Chozas, 16
05001 Avila
tel: (18)211340
62 rooms - Pts 8,500
Credit cards: all major
Restaurant
U.S. Rep: NIC Tours
Rep tel: (415) 871-6680
Nearest airport: Madrid (113 km)
Nearest train station: Avila

The Colón is a stately hotel with some elegant touches, built in 1950 right in the middle of the enchanting Gothic Quarter (Barrio Gótico) of Barcelona.   The lobby is entered up a broad, cream-carpeted stairway which passes through an impressive, square stone arch.   The decor here, as throughout the hotel's public rooms, is perfectly lovely and makes you want to linger to watch the passersby in front of the massive cathedral across the street.   On certain days local folklore buffs gather for a session of the regional dance, the sardanya (ask at the hotel desk for the current schedule).   Some thirty-four of its rooms overlook the city's famous cathedral - a few have terraces.   When making reservations request a room with a terrace, preferably a quieter location on one of the upper floors, and, if the budget allows, a suite or double room with a sitting area, for more money but also more space.   All of the rooms have wonderful high ceilings and are accented with old-world touches which lend an intimate feeling to this fairly big hotel.   The Colón is a good, middle-of-the-road choice between the other two hotels mentioned here, and enjoys an incomparable location.

HOTEL COLON
Avenida de la Catedral, 7
08002 Barcelona
tel: (3)3011404 telex: 52654
fax: 3172915
166 rooms - Pts 11,600
Credit cards: all major
Restaurant
Nearest airport: Barcelona
Nearest train station: Barcelona

Within easy walking distance of the "Ramblas" and the Gothic Quarter, this is a delightful hospice in the middle of the hustle and bustle of Barcelona. Originally the palace of a very wealthy 19th century woman, the patron of San Juan Bosco, an Italian ambiance pervades the decor. It has a rooftop garden (a rare treasure) off a simply beautiful bar/lounge which boasts a sculpted ceiling, parquet floors and abundant antiques. Although the rooms are neither large nor lavish, each is unique in dimension and furnishings, has sculpted walls and a high ceiling. The rooms are centered around an interior arched gallery, topped with a beautiful old stained-glass skylight and accessed by an exquisite central staircase. To avoid street noise, you might want to request a room overlooking the terrace and, if you are there in the summertime, be sure to specify air conditioning. The Gran Vía is a very special hotel in a special city, offering the intimacy and service that only a small, well-run family establishment can. It has no restaurant, but many excellent ones are nearby. And for a large city hotel the price is exceptional.

HOTEL GRAN VIA
Gran Vía, 642
08007 Barcelona
tel: (3)3181900
48 rooms - Pts 7,100
Credit cards: all major
No restaurant
Nearest airport: Barcelona
Nearest train station: Barcelona

"Ritz" denotes luxury and this lovely old lady lives up to her name. The 1919 hotel has recently undergone extensive remodeling and the old rooms have only gained in ambiance. The molded French-style walls are painted in soft colors and climb to ceilings that are at least 15 feet high. The bedrooms are immense by modern hotel standards, and furnished handsomely in old-world style - what the Spanish call "al gran estilo". Salvador Dali's favorite room, and ours, is number 110, with a sunken Roman bath and its bed tucked into an alcove. The renovation of the Hotel Ritz's public rooms is masterful, and the resulting lobby, central hall, lounges and excellent restaurants are elegant without being intimidating. Manager Alfonso Jordán takes justifiable pride in his loyal and dedicated staff because the service is nothing short of perfect and the English-speaking concierges go out of their way to anticipate your needs - a real asset in this city with so much to offer. You will feel pampered at the Ritz and that is a feeling hard to come by in large city hotels these days.

HOTEL RITZ
Gran Vía de les Corts Catalanes, 668
08010 Barcelona
tel: (3)31852-00 telex: 52739
fax: 3180148
171 rooms - Pts 35,500
Credit cards: all major
Restaurant
U.S. Rep: NIC Tours
Rep tel: (415) 871-6680
Nearest airport: Barcelona
Nearest train station: Barcelona

This fortress parador on the sea is undoubtedly one of the most remarkable in Spain. Isolated on a craggy point beyond the little fishing village of Bayona, it is encircled by the ramparts of the former fortress of Monte Real, which protect it on three sides from the wild, crashing sea. The bedrooms are large and charmingly furnished, with wooden floors and ceilings. Request well in advance a room with a view to the sea to fully appreciate the beauty of this popular spot. Room number 102 - with its circular corner balcony, private sitting room and four-poster canopy beds - is spectacular and worth the splurge. Lovely antiques are as at home here and throughout the hotel as the comfortable, traditional wood and leather Spanish furniture. With its massive stone stairway and original stone, domed ceiling the lobby is stunning and an interior patio with its fountain is delightful. An elegant dining room is found off the lobby and a more informal tavern, "La Pinta", is located on the grounds and overlooks the sea. Several days could easily be enjoyed in this romantic, luxurious hotel with its dramatic backdrop of the clear Atlantic Ocean.

P.N. CONDE DE GONDOMAR
36300 Bayona, Pontevedra
tel: (86)355000
128 rooms - Pts 11,000
Credit cards: all major
Restaurant, pool, tennis
U.S. Rep: NIC Tours
Rep tel: (415) 871-6680
Nearest airport: Vigo (21 km)
Nearest train station: Vigo (21 km)

This 12th century palace on the edge of a sleepy village was practically devastated by the French in 1808 but was rescued and restored by the government as a historical monument. The royal family of Ferdinand and Isabella stayed at this delightful hotel on their pilgrimage to Santiago. Of the original castle, there remains only the Torreón, which can be visited on Friday afternoons. The tower bar, located in the cellar and remarkably reconstructed from the original foundation, is reached down a narrow stone stairway, whose thick stone walls are draped with colorful tapestries, and whose vaulted, painted, thirty-six foot high wooden ceiling has massive beams that support a huge, antique iron chandelier. Another highlight is the fabulous mudejar ceiling in the Salón Artesonado, brought here from the town of San Román del Valle in León and lovingly reassembled. The spacious bedrooms flank long, whitewashed hallways lined with antique benches, and have a rustic, almost "western" ambiance, with tile floors and leather furnishings. They have lovely views of the town and countryside, and those on the upper floor have terraces.

P.N. REY FERNANDO II DE LEON
49600 Benavente, Zamora
tel: (88)630300
30 rooms - Pts 8,000
Credit cards: all major
Restaurant
U.S. Rep: NIC Tours
Rep tel: (415) 871-6680
Nearest airport: Valladolid (90 km)
Nearest train station: Zamora (60 km)

This remarkable "highway inn" has been a lifetime labor of love for Señor and Señora Landa, both artists, who opened a restaurant on this spot in 1958, then the hotel in 1964. Reception and some suites (in which the King and Queen of Spain have stayed) are found in a 14th century tower - with broad marble staircase and Toledan ceiling - brought here from its original location 20 kilometers away. Standing in the front courtyard is a music pavilion that was once in the main plaza in Burgos. The Landa Palace is a treasure trove of antiques and collectibles from all over Spain: copper pots, water jugs, irons, scales, fashions and seventy-five clocks. The dining room is breathtaking: tall single tapers grace the tables beneath a bóveda ceiling and a suspended fifteen foot iron chandelier. Served by the "fastest waiters in Spain", the cuisine of Chef Pérez is among the best in the country; his gazpacho and house tinto wine outstanding. Overlooking the courtyard or countryside, each bedroom is unique and spacious, accented with wood, colorful carpets and bedspreads. The Landa is a tranquil haven just a mile from the bustle of Burgos.

HOTEL LANDA PALACE
Carretera de Madrid, km. 236
09000 Burgos
tel: (47)206343 telex: 39534
fax: 264676
42 rooms - Pts 13,900
Credit cards: VS, MC
Restaurant, indoor/ outdoor pool
U.S. Rep: David Mitchell
Rep tel: 800-372-1323
Nearest airport: Vitoria (112 km)
Nearest train station: Burgos (2 km)

One of the most dramatic paradors in the country, the Duques de Cardona has dominated the fortified town of Cardona for centuries from its 1500-foot-high hilltop setting.   This spot was chosen as a home by the Duke in the 10th century and, although much of the construction is recent, the period flavor and restoration have been faithfully attended to.   Behind the hotel is a unique 2nd century tower and 11th century church along with a beautiful Roman patio from which a "bird's eye" view is obtainable of the unusual salt hills, the pueblo and the Pyrenees.   The bedrooms are ample in size with wine-red tile floors, colorful woven bedspreads and dark wooden furniture.   Room number 705 has "Catalan" beds with illustrated headboards, and overlooks the town and the ancient tower.   Rooms 607 and 609 are semi-suites, and are divine, with curtained, canopied beds and wonderful perspectives onto the patio.   The restaurant is spectacularly situated in a forever-long, stone-arched and wooden-beamed hall. Although out of the way, this parador offers a memorable night's stay in a carefully renovated historical setting with all the modern comforts of home.

P.N. DUQUES DE CARDONA
Castillo
08261 Cardona, Barcelona
tel: (3)8691275
fax: 8691636
61 rooms - Pts 7,000
Credit cards: all major
Restaurant, medieval castle
U.S. Rep: NIC Tours
Rep tel: (415) 871-6680
Nearest airport: Barcelona (99 km)
Nearest train station: Manresa (32 km)

This hotel is ideally located in a small, ancient village, imbued with medieval ambiance but still only thirty minutes from downtown Seville. Of the three castles built in the walled town of Carmona, one was converted into this parador in 1976. Formerly decorated by the same Moorish architects responsible for the famous Alcázar in Seville, the restoration has preserved the original Moslem flavor while adding rather more modern appointments. You will be charmed from the beginning by the entry through the castle gate into the courtyard surrounded by the restored castle walls. Entry into the building itself transports you into the Moorish past by the fantastic patio with its tile floor, impressive fountain and slender, graceful arches and columns. You will be delighted by the intricately patterned, colorful ceramic-tile decor throughout the hotel. The large guest rooms maintain the reliable parador high standards, decorated in traditional Spanish style. For just a few dollars more, request one of the twelve rooms with a terrace - and feast your eyes on the wonderful view from the hilltop vantage point over the vast plains below. The same panorama can be enjoyed from the terrace outside the pleasant little bar.

P.N. ALCAZAR DEL REY DON PEDRO
41410 Carmona, Sevilla
tel: (54)141010
59 rooms - Pts 10,500
Credit cards: all major
Restaurant, pool
U.S. Rep: NIC Tours
Rep tel: (415) 871-6680
Nearest airport: Seville (25 km)
Nearest train station: Seville (38 km)

Imaginatively and extensively renovated, this relatively recent addition to the parador chain is a member of the select group that merits four stars. It is located just off the main plaza in the charming, historic town of Chinchón (justifiably famous for its anis liqueur). The plaza, with its many overhanging wood balconies (and still used for bullfights), is very picturesque. Installed in a 17th-century Augustine monastery, fountains, hanging and terraced gardens, reflecting pools, and worn-stone patios soothe the secular guest here with the same tranquility once treasured by its previous religious residents. The pale-brick-paved central cloister features a glass-enclosed colonnade, lined with antiques and hung with tapestries. The guestrooms are simple and lovely, floored in red tile, with whitewashed walls and colorful wooden beds topped with cream-colored spreads. The rooms in *la parte vieja* overlooking the garden are particularly attractive, and room 8, with a private sitting room and balcony is superior for not too many more pesetas. The cheerful dining room is accented with colorful *azulejos* and offers an interesting variety of dishes. Try to fit in a visit to the historic restaurant Mesón Cuevas de Vino at the top of town, well-known locally for its traditional grills and sangría.

P.N. DE CHINCHON
Avenida Generalísimo, 1
28370 Chinchón, Madrid
tel: (1)8940836 telex: 49398
fax: 8940908
38 rooms - Pts 10,000
Credit cards: all major
U.S. rep: NIC Tours
Rep tel: (415) 871-6680
Nearest airport: Madrid (45 km)
Nearest train station: Aranjuez (21 km)

The grounds of this parador include acres of grassy hillside, a huge blue swimming pool that overlooks the city and tree-shaded areas ideal for cool walks on hot days - very inviting for travelers who simply want to relax and spend time in the sun. Being of the modern persuasion, this parador does not have the usual antique ambiance. That is certainly not to say that it is not attractive, however. The public rooms seem to cover almost as many acres as the lawn and command spectacular views of the valley and the city. Appointments are equally modern with occasional tapestries and old-style chandeliers to remind you of the past. The spacious bedrooms are similarly furnished in contemporary Spanish style, and for a 10% surcharge you can procure a room with the same gorgeous view you see from the lobby and dining room - over the lawn and trees to the city below. The vista is especially attractive at night. All this natural (and man-made) air-conditioned luxury is still only 15 minutes - by car or taxi - from the Mezquita and the fascinating and colorful old Jewish Quarter.

P.N. DE LA ARRUZAFA
Carretera de El Brillante N
Avenida de la Arruzafa, s/n
14012 Córdoba
tel: (57)275900
95 rooms - Pts 10,500
Credit cards: all major
Restaurant, pool, tennis
U.S. Rep: NIC Tours
Rep tel: (415) 871-6680
Nearest airport: Córdoba
Nearest train station: Córdoba

Named for the brilliant 12th century Jewish philosopher who was born in Córdoba, the Maimónides advertises itself as being only four meters from the famous Mezquita. Indeed, when we looked out our window, it seemed we could reach out and touch it. With a prime location at the center of the crowded old quarter, the inexpensive parking garage under the hotel is a wonderful convenience. The decor of the public rooms is an unusual but inviting mixture of Spanish modern and lovely antiques: chests, suits of armor, religious paintings and sculpture. An intimate glass-enclosed garden patio adds to the welcoming feeling as does the friendly, competent, English-speaking staff. The moderate-sized rooms are comfortable in a regional-style decor, with wood and leather furniture, drapes and bedspreads in subdued colors, and air conditioning. Although there is no restaurant in the hotel, breakfast is served in the bar off the lobby, and there are two neighboring restaurants to select from: the excellent Caballo Rojo across the street and the Mesón Bandolero around the corner in the palace where Maimonides' Arabic counterpart, Averroes, was born.

HOTEL MAIMONIDES
Torrijos, 4
14003 Córdoba
tel: (57)471500 telex: 76594
90 rooms - Pts 11,400
Credit cards: all major
No restaurant
Nearest airport: Córdoba
Nearest train station: Córdoba

In the foothills of the justifiably famous Picos de Europa, nestled atop the tiny mountain town of Covadonga, is the peaceful Hotel Pelayo. The hotel is sandwiched between the striking neo-Roman basilica and the cave of the Virgin of Asturias, which attract thousands of sightseers every year. Built in 1919 as a mountain retreat and hunting lodge, the inn has been remodeled recently. Though not elegant, the rooms are comfortable and clean, and the setting unsurpassed in beauty. This is where Generalísimo Franco came to relax and hunt, and always reserved for him was a corner double with views to both the basilica and the deep green mountains. The rooms are nicely decorated, with red tones predominant, and have rustic wooden furnishings and floors and quite large, modern baths. All of the doubles have lovely vistas; a few rooms on the second floor have terraces, as do those on the third floor. There is an attractive lounge and bar on the first floor, but the restaurant is fairly ordinary. We suggest you head for the hills and the glacial lake Enol with a picnic, as the scenery ranks among the most spectacular in the country.

HOTEL PELAYO
33589 Covadonga, Asturias
tel: (85)846000
43 rooms - Pts 7,560
Closed: Christmas to January 1
Credit cards: VS, MC
Restaurant
Nearest airport: Avilés (110 km)
Nearest train station: Arriondas (15 km)

During its history, this charming hospice has been converted from a 16th century wayside inn to a convent, to a farmhouse and most recently back to an inn. In typical Spanish fashion, the whitewashed building forms a square around a bright interior patio with fountain and flowers, and a wood-beamed gallery. A small dining room off the patio offers unusually good fare and on summer evenings there is music and a barbecue on the back terrace. It is located only seven kilometers from the enchanting town of Cuenca, with its hanging houses, and only an hour and a half from Madrid, but the atmosphere is most definitely country, with cool breezes from the nearby Huécar river carrying the smell of pines and the sound of birds into every corner of the hotel. All of the bedrooms have countryside or patio views, and the tile floors, wooden ceilings and traditional, pale wood furnishings are much as they might have been over two centuries ago, the only discordant note being the rather flowery drapes and spreads. Room number 130 is particularly nice, a spacious suite with a fireplace and charming, old-fashioned sitting room. The ambiance is familial and the service personal in this intimate hideaway.

HOTEL CUEVA DEL FRAILE
Carretera de Buenache, km. 7
16001 Cuenca
tel: (66)211571
54 rooms - Pts 5,500
Closed: January 10 to March 1
Credit cards: VS MC
Restaurant, pool, tennis courts
Nearest airport: Madrid (165 km)
Nearest train station: Cuenca (7 km)

The stately Hotel Victoria Palace, with its English country-manor flavor, is located a stone's throw from one of the most popular tourist attractions in Spain, yet offers a quiet and luxurious refuge from El Escorial's daytrippers and the fast-lane pace of Madrid. To see the whole monastery-cum-palace properly, you will need two visits, and this hotel will make that a pleasant prospect. A welcoming garden cafe in front (seemingly created for the turn-of-the-century tea-drinking crowd) entices you into the marble-floored lobby and up a graceful brass-railed double stairway to a spacious lounge with cozy brocade chairs, rich wood panelling and corner fireplace. Upstairs, past wide landings dappled with sunlight streaming through stained glass, are tastefully appointed bedrooms with lofty, high ceilings, polished wood floors and large windows overlooking the gardens. The service, though a bit formal, is correct and knowledgeable. By contrast, the warmly intimate, pub-style bar is charming and friendly. This impressive hotel, with its unique spired roof, will enhance a trip to Felipe II's palace.

HOTEL VICTORIA PALACE
Juan Toledo, 4
28200 San Lorenzo de El Escorial, Madrid
tel: (1)8901511 telex: 22227
85 rooms - Pts 8,200
Credit cards: all major
Restaurant, pool
U.S. Rep: NIC Tours
Rep tel: (415) 871-6680
Nearest airport: Madrid (46 km)
Nearest train station: El Escorial

At the border of the Basque country, Fuenterrabía (in Basque, Hondarribia) boasts one of Spain's most original paradors. Installed in a 12th century castle, the imposing stone edifice has been occupied and personalized by Ferdinand and Isabella and their grandson Charles V, Emperor of the Holy Roman Empire. Its incredible nine-foot-thick walls have withstood countless assaults over the centuries and today offer unique shelter, along with such comforts as minibars and maid service. An outstanding feature of the Emperador is its wonderful stone-paved lobby, featuring lances, cannon, suits of armor, tapestries and a remarkable, soaring fifty-foot ceiling, overlooked through stone arches by a cozy first-floor lounge with a beamed ceiling. Renovated in 1983 are sixteen individually decorated rooms, all with wood floors and stone ceilings, and each one handsomely furnished in dark wood and accented with deep earth colors. It is important to secure reservations well in advance as this intimate, medieval inn, situated only a block from the sea, in a well-preserved and perfectly charming medieval town, is very popular.

P.N. EL EMPERADOR
Plaza de Armas
20280 Fuenterrabía, Guipúzcoa
tel: (43)642140
16 rooms - Pts 9,500
Credit cards: all major
No restaurant, medieval castle
U.S. Rep: NIC Tours
Rep tel: (415) 871-6680
Nearest airport: San Sebastian (2 km)
Nearest train station: Irun (5 km)

The parador in Granada is in a class by itself, but it must be reserved months in advance and it cannot compete with the setting and views afforded by the Alhambra Palace.   The Palace is located in the Alhambra, preferable to downtown, and to be able to gaze out from your room over the Alhambra, the cathedral and the historic city through Moorish-arched windows is an opportunity with which the parador cannot compete.   Opened in 1910, this has long been a mainstay of the Alhambra hotels.   Andrés Segovia, the famous Spanish guitarist, played his first concert here, and it remains a favorite hotel choice in Granada for most visiting dignitaries. The decor of the public rooms is enchantingly, almost overwhelmingly, Moorish - from the intricately carved ceilings, unusual decorative touches, to the symmetrically placed, arched doorways and colorful tiled walls.   The bedrooms are large and comfortable (the Andrés Segovia suite magnificent) and most have been recently remodeled.   The hotel is air-conditioned - a blessing in Granada's hot summer months.   Savor one of the best views in Spain from the expansive bar area or on the outdoor terrace.

HOTEL ALHAMBRA PALACE
Peña Partida, 2
18009 Granada
tel: (58)221468 telex: 78400
145 rooms - Pts 12,000
Credit cards: all major
Restaurant
U.S. Rep: NIC Tours
Rep tel: (415) 871-6680
Nearest airport: Granada
Nearest train station: Granada

For those travelers who enjoy being in the heart of town, the Juan Miguel offers an attractive and relatively economical alternative to the hotels located above Granada near the Alhambra. Situated in the Puerta Real, smack in the Centro and only a couple of blocks from the lovely Bib-Ramblas square, the hotel is just a few minutes by foot from all of the major attractions in this charming city, and a quick cab ride - or an invigorating walk - from the Alhambra. Behind its handsome white facade, the Juan Miguel is intimate in atmosphere and modern in appointments. The small lobby, lounge and bar area fairly sparkle, from the white marble floors to the brightly colored couches and easy chairs. The guestrooms upstairs are sound-proofed, amply proportioned and pleasantly decorated in earthtones with contemporary wood furnishings. Adding to its choice of two restaurants which, although we didn't same the fare, seemed appealing and reasonable priced. Granada features much more than the beautiful Moorish palace on the hill, and the Juan Miguel puts its many attractions at your doorstep.

HOTEL JUAN MIGUEL
Acera del Darro, 24
(Puerta Real)
18005 Granada
tel: (58)258912 telex: 78527
66 rooms - Pts 8,300
Credit cards: all major
Restaurants, garage
Nearest airport: Granada
Nearest train station: Granada

This is Spain's most famous and popular parador, and as a result reservations must be secured at least six to eight months in advance. Installed in a 16th century convent, restoration has been directed so as to retain much of the original structure, including the chapel where Queen Isabella was first buried before being moved to the cathedral downtown. Outside, lovely Alhambra-style gardens and walks blend well with the neighboring marvel. Inside, the decor is a mixture of Moorish and Christian. The former shows up in wonderful ceilings, carved doors, ceramic tile, and the graceful arches in the beautiful interior patio. The public rooms are rich in antique religious art objects - paintings, sculpture and colorful tapestries. The guest rooms are comfortably unostentatious, with period accents and views varying from excellent to ordinary. The dining room is in a style apart - its walls are lined with handsome contemporary abstract paintings. An outstanding feature of the parador is its secluded location within the Alhambra - an oasis of calm in the usually bustling tourist area - which is indeed appealing.

P.N. SAN FRANCISCO
Alhambra
18009 Granada
tel: (58)221441 telex: 78792
fax: 222264
39 rooms - Pts 14,500
Credit cards: all major
Restaurant, 16th century convent
U.S. Rep: NIC Tours
Rep tel: (415) 871-6680
Nearest airport: Granada
Nearest train station: Granada

Shadowed by the famous monastery's towers, this inn was a Hieronymite hospital and pharmacy in the 16th century, but, since the days of Ferdinand and Isabella, has sheltered those who came to worship. Until 1960 visitors exchanged a daily donation of a mere 50 pesetas for accommodation. Still today, for value received and atmosphere, follow the footsteps of the faithful to this inn, as there is nothing comparable in Guadalupe, or anywhere else. Sharing and managing the edifice is an active Franciscan religious order, whose guides regularly conduct an insider's tour of their monastery, museum and cathedral - a crazy and wonderful mixture of mudejar and Gothic architecture. The hotel rooms overlook the original stone-arched and paved hospital patio. Their decor varies wildly - some incredible, but all adequate and all with baths. To stay here is to live and breathe the history of Spain. Request a room on the gallery; number 112 is especially nice - given to visiting religious notables; the 2nd-floor corner suite (no number) is Baroquely elegant and many 3rd-floor rooms boast original mudéjar ceilings. Delicious fare and homemade wine is served under a high wooden ceiling in a richly paneled dining room.

HOSPEDERIA EL REAL MONASTERIO
Plaza S.M. Juan Carlos I
10140 Guadalupe, Cáceres
tel: (27)367000
40 rooms - Pts 4,400
Credit cards: VS
Restaurant, ancient monastery
Nearest airport: Madrid (225 km)
Nearest train station: Talavera (130 km)

Built in the 14th century as a hospital to shelter and minister to pilgrims who came to venerate the famous Black Virgin of Guadalupe, this parador now provides admirably for the needs of the modern-day visitor. It is located directly across the street from the Franciscan monastery in a village from which the Catholic monarchs granted permission for Columbus' ships to depart for the New World. Whitewashed, with red roof tiles, the Zurbarán - named after a famous 17th century painter - invites you to enjoy its cool, Moorish gardens sheltering a sparkling turquoise pool, and to dine on its outdoor terrace overlooking a tiled, mudéjar fountain. Thanks to the local craftsmen, colorful tile is found throughout the hotel: the interior patio is especially lovely. Recently remodeled, the parador has added twenty new rooms which maintain the period ambiance faithfully and all have garden-view terraces. However, the old rooms with low, stone doorways are still the favorites - some with canopied beds, fireplaces and balconies (ask for "una habitación antigua con terraza"). But, no matter the room, this is a special inn in a tranquil and picturesque locale.

P.N. ZURBARAN
Marqués de la Romana, 10
10140 Guadalupe, Cáceres
tel: (27)367075
40 rooms - Pts 8,000
Credit cards: all major
Restaurant, pool
U.S. Rep: NIC Tours
Rep tel: (415) 871-6680
Nearest airport: Madrid (225 km)
Nearest train station: Talavera (130 km)

This engaging parador crowns the Cerro (hill) de Santa Catalina, who is the patron saint of Jaén, and flanks the Moorish castle after which it is named and whose architecture it imitates. It is immediately apparent that much imaginative effort went into the construction of this "copycat" castle-hotel. The public rooms feature tapestry-hung stone-brick walls that soar to carved-wood or arched-granite ceilings, cavernous fireplaces and recessed windows. The high-ceilinged guestrooms are spacious and bright, with rough-hewn brick floors trimmed in green tile, leather and wood furniture, cheery spreads and throw-rugs, and shiny green-and-white tiled baths. Each has a roomy terrace that commands panoramic vistas over the city, the fertile Guadalquivir river valley, and an endless expanse of undulating hills studded with the olive groves for which this region is renowned. Tranquil will define your stay here, which should be combined with a visit to the Arab baths and the barrio de Magdalena in town.

P.N. CASTILLO DE SANTA CATALINA
23001 Jaén
tel: (53)264411
fax: 223930
45 rooms - Pts 9,000
Credit cards: all major
Extensive countryside views, pool
U.S. Rep: NIC Tours
Rep tel: (415) 871-6680
Nearest airport: Granada (90 km)
Nearest train station: Jaén

In the 15th century, the Counts of Oropesa built a fortress surrounded by gardens in the hillside town of Jarandilla above the fertile, tobacco-growing Tiétar valley. Their noble home is now the Carlos V, beautifully preserved, with odd-shaped towers, ramparts and a drawbridge completing the late-medieval picture. The cool, stone-paved inner courtyard has ivy-covered walls and a placid central pool, overlooked by a terraced second floor lounge with a magnificent fireplace and lovely antiques. There are 16 guestrooms in the original building, and an additional 37 in a modern annex behind, all pleasantly decorated with dark wooden furniture, cream spreads and drapes and brick-red tiles. The spacious high ceilings, rich wood floors and antique furnishings of the castle chambers lend an atmosphere impossible to duplicate. The recent addition of a swimming pool and tennis facilities have only enhanced this charming hilltop hideaway.

P.N. CARLOS V
Carretera de Plasencia
10450 Jarandilla de la Vera, Cáceres
tel: (27)560117
53 rooms - Pts 8,500
Credit cards: all major
Restaurant, pool, tennis
U.S. Rep: NIC Tours
Rep tel: (415) 871-6680
Nearest airport: Madrid (213 km)
Nearest train station: Navalmoral (30 km)

The San Marcos, recently added to parador chain, is elegantly installed in what was originally an elaborate stone monastery commissioned by Ferdinand (the Catholic king) at the beginning of the 16th century. Before its conversion to a hotel in 1965, it was used as a military prison and stable that saw lots of activity during the Civil War. Its immense façade is deceptive as there are only thirty-five rooms in the historical part of the edifice (referred to as the *zona noble*). The rest of the space is occupied by an exquisite stone patio peopled with statues of saints, an archaeological museum, a chapel, spacious lounges and hallways lavishly furnished with antiques, and a modern restaurant offering a delectable menu (the scallops, or *vieira*, are superb). The old rooms are discovered off a maze of creaky, worn hallways and are large and comfortable, with high ceilings, old-world ambiance and antique furnishings. The suites overlooking the entrance are a treat: enormous and secured behind walls now centuries old. The rooms in the new addition will not disappoint; they are quiet, maintain a traditional Spanish flavor and overlook a lovely interior garden. The San Marcos is steeped in history and has a gracious staff.

HOSTAL SAN MARCOS
Plaza San Marcos, 7
24001 León
tel: (87)237300 telex: 89809
253 rooms - Pts 11,500
Credit cards: all major
Restaurant, 16th century monastery
U.S. Rep: NIC Tours
Rep tel: (415) 871-6680
Nearest airport: Valladolid (139 km)
Nearest train station: León

This select hotel is an experience unto itself, spectacularly situated on over 1,000 acres of scenic countryside. No detail has been overlooked to offer every convenience in a distinctive atmosphere combining characteristic Andalusian style with contemporary elegance. Graceful Moorish arches, carved-wood ceilings, tiled patios, grilled terraces, marble fountains and blossoming gardens surround the pampered guest in this intimate hideaway located just north of Salinas (between Granada and Antequera) on C344. A sampling of the services that come with the pricey accommodation here is: fitness equipment and programs, saunas, jacuzzi, golf (by summer 1990), tennis, fishing, hunting, horseback riding, climbing, indoor and magnificent outdoor pools, concerts, breakfast, and a staff that outnumbers the clientele. Each spacious guestroom is unique, richly and imaginatively decorated in soft colors, with large bathrooms (featuring both bath and shower), and either balconies or garden patios from which you can enjoy the tranquil landscape. The orientation of rooms 1-6 (doubles with sitting room) and 7 and 10 (doubles) provides them with particularly ample upstairs terraces. In addition you have your choice of three dining spots, one of which, La Finca, has gained justifiable regional renown.

HOTEL LA BOBADILLA
Apartado 52
18006 Loja, Granada
tel: (58)321861 telex: 78732
fax: 321810
35 rooms - Pts 28,700
Credit cards: all major
Unique setting
Nearest airport: Granada (55 km)
Nearest train station: Bobadilla (40 km)

Over thirty years ago, on a hilltop in a tiny fishing village on the Mediterranean, a gracious manor house was built. Today the village is a seaside resort whose population swells to three times its number during the summer, and the house has become a stylish hotel, still offering treasured peace and quiet on the Costa Brava, yet only 10 minutes by footpath to the beach.   The whitewashed inn, draped in ivy and bougainvilla, has a pretty Andalusian patio in front, a delightful terrace out back with an attractive pool, bar and first-class restaurant overlooking Lloret's rooftops to the sparkling sea.   The public rooms are charming, with marble floors and antique touches, and the service is warm and accommodating.   Although all of the roomy bedrooms are comfortable and pleasant (if a bit too modern), in general their decor is unexceptional.   However, there are fourteen rooms in the original building, and those with sitting rooms and stone terraces and/or views to the ocean are worth the additional expense.   The location is unbeatable, and the Roger de Flor an appealing alternative to the costly, crowded and noisy Costa Brava beachfront hotels.

HOTEL ROGER DE FLOR
Turo de L'estelat s/n
17310 Lloret de Mar, Gerona
tel: (72)364800 telex: 57173
100 rooms - Pts 18,600*
 * includes half-pension for two
Open March through December
Credit cards: all major
U.S. Rep: NIC Tours
Rep tel: (415) 871-6680
Nearest airport: Barcelona (67 km)
Nearest train station: Blanes (6 km)

This delightful hotel is on several floors of a large building in the heart of Madrid. Two elevators service the different floors, and the one on the right - a tiny, five-sided affair - is unique, obviously having been constructed to fit the precise space available.   Found on the third floor (Spanish second) are an extremely inviting reception, lobby and restaurant area whose decorative style could be called intense: pseudo-French with antique accents.   But it is spacious, attractive and cozy, and a veritable oasis in the heart of town.   The cozy bedrooms, each different in shape and size, are elaborately decorated with matching fabrics and offer old-world ambiance coupled with modern amenities.   Manager Antonio Gil is justifiably proud of the frequent maintenance schedule - no chipped paint or worn carpet anywhere.   The owners have gone to great lengths to soundproof the hotel from the noises of Madrid's central street, Gran Vía.   The hotel is a few blocks from the chic Puerta del Sol, a shopper's paradise, and the Plaza Mayor with its charming cafes.   The Arosa is an excellent value for quality received.

HOTEL AROSA
Salud, 21
28013 Madrid
tel: (1)5321600 telex: 43618
fax: 5313127
126 rooms - Pts 9,950
Credit cards: all major
Restaurant
U.S. Rep: NIC Tours
Rep tel: (415) 871-6680
Nearest airport: Madrid
Nearest train station: Madrid

If you want to be able to luxuriate around a tree-ringed pool in the countryside when you are not sightseeing in the big city, then you will be enchanted by this lovely spot.   In these tranquil grounds you will feel far from the hustle and bustle of Spain's largest city - but you are less than ten minutes by cab or car from the center of town, in Madrid's exclusive residential area of Puerta de Hierro. Although from the outside the building appears somewhat ordinary, inside, the spacious public areas are appealingly furnished with classical overstuffed couches and chairs and gorgeous oriental rugs.   Many beautiful original art works and impressive tapestries add considerably to the charm.   In addition to the pleasant dining room, there is a very attractive little terrace restaurant overlooking the pool. The bedrooms are equally spacious and comfortable.   If you request it, you will love one of the rooms that faces the pool surrounded by pretty lawns and trees. The furnishings are pleasantly old-world in style although not antiques.   If you want to combine relaxing in the country with sampling the lively life of the cosmopolitan city, you cannot come closer than this.

HOTEL MONTE REAL
Arroyofresno, 19
28035 Madrid
tel: (1)2162140 telex: 22089
fax: 2162140
80 rooms - Pts 22,000
Credit cards: AX VS DC
Restaurant, pool
Nearest airport: Madrid
Nearest train station: Madrid

Frequently referred to as one of the world's top ten hotels, The Ritz, across the street from the Prado Museum, is all one could ask for in a hotel - except inexpensive.   The opulent old-world decor has been restored under the watchful eye of the executive director, John M. Macedo, and creates a *"Belle Epoque"* ambiance.   The restoration is based on considerable research to ensure that the decor recreates exactly its 1910 glory.   A statue of Diana which had graced the upper hall bar was retrieved, restored and replaced where it had stood for the first forty years of the hotel's existence.   The expanse of lobby and grand hall behind it are magnificent.   The restaurant, which features regional specialties, is hung with dramatic tapestries that were refurbished by the original makers, the Royal Tapestry Factory.   The bedrooms are spectacular in their decor and the same glorious hand-woven carpet that adorns the rest of the hotel has been woven to fit each one.   Everything, from the striking gold bathroom fixtures (with giant showerheads that make it seem like you are standing in a gentle rain) to the tasteful and handsome furnishings, will make you feel pampered.   The Ritz successfully combines the luxury of the contemporary world, with turn-of-the century elegance.

THE RITZ
Plaza de la Lealtad, 5
28014 Madrid
tel: (1)5212857 telex: 43986
fax: 5328776
176 rooms - Pts 44,000
Credit cards: all major
Indoor & outdoor restaurants
U.S. Rep: NIC Tours
Rep tel: (415) 871-6680
Nearest airport: Madrid
Nearest train station: Madrid

Location and value are two of the best reasons for choosing this old-timer. It is located about halfway between the lively center of town at the Puerta del Sol and the elegant Paseo del Prado where the fabulous Museo del Prado awaits your visit. At the same time, the immediate vicinity of the hotel encompasses the relatively tranquil, pretty little plaza of Santa Ana, near the concentration of antique stores that line the Calle del Prado. Built in 1925, the hotel reflects its origins. The ground-floor entry from which the concierge efficiently directs the bustling scene is rather plain. The front desk, lobby and restaurant are found one floor up: removing the public rooms from city street noise. The bedrooms are on the floors above the lobby. They are all comfortable and the better rooms, facing the Plaza Santa Ana, are steeped with real old-world charm and style. A tiny, barely practicable, glassed-in terrace looks over the typical little plaza. The hotel is air-conditioned throughout - very welcome during a hot Madrid summer. The Gran Hotel Victoria, recently refurbished, is one of the best values in town and within walking distance of many of the highlights.

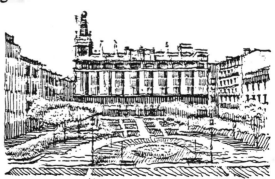

GRAN HOTEL VICTORIA
Plaza del Angel, 7
28012 Madrid
tel: (1)2314500 telex: 42920
fax: 3143156
200 rooms - Pts 8,100
Credit cards: all major
Restaurant
Nearest airport: Madrid
Nearest train station: Madrid

Situated on Mount Gibralfaro, high above the sprawling port city of Málaga, this parador of the same name commands a stunning view. Installed in what looks like an old stone mansion with wrought-iron grilles and arcaded wraparound galleries, the hotel is surrounded by hillside greenery and located within easy walking distance of a ruined Moorish fortress. Unadorned comfort describes the accommodation offered here. The twin-bedded, air-conditioned rooms are all the same: of average size, though with ample baths, warm-red tile floors, textured, whitewashed walls, traditional wood furnishings with leather accents, and a diminutive sitting area. Each has a small brick balcony that juts into the room and out over the hilltop, providing the guests with personal space from which to enjoy the panorama that leads down to the sea. This vista is also available from the terraces off the restaurant and bar (which have separate menus), making them extremely appealing dining spots during warm weather, as evidenced by the number of locals who make the trip up the mountain to eat. This tiny, attractive parador provides a convenient stopping place along the Costa del Sol, but be sure to reserve well in advance during high season.

P.N. DE GIBRALFARO
29016 Málaga
tel: (52)221903
fax: 221902
12 rooms - Pts 9,000
Credit cards: all major
Panoramic city view
U.S. Rep: NIC Tours
Rep tel: (415) 871-6680
Nearest airport: Málaga
Nearest train station: Málaga

The ancient seignorial mansion which now houses the Emperatriz was constructed at the end of the 16th century, and has hosted such illustrious guests as the Empress Isabel of Portugal and Felipes II and III. The hotel is located on Mérida's lively, stone-arcaded main square and, judging by the number of patrons, its pretty outdoor terrace cafe, with red-upholstered, white wrought-iron furniture, is a popular gathering spot. When you enter the manor, your first view will be of the wonderful cloistered central patio - with slender pillars and graceful arches - set up to allow you to dine in a truly noble setting. Everything about the hotel, from its fabulous historic facade, to its majestic stairway winding up to a stone-arcaded gallery, appears perfect for our taste. Unfortunately, due to "hotelocracy" in the absence of the director, we were unable to see the rooms personally. However, based on our impressions of everything else we feel confident that the integrity of the decor is maintained throughout, and this hotel offers such a good value that we have included it anyway. In this ancient city - Spain's richest in Roman remains - you cannot go wrong in the Emperatriz; the setting is charming and the location superb.

HOTEL EMPERATRIZ
Plaza de España
06800 Mérida, Badajoz
tel: (24)313111
44 rooms - Pts 5,850
Credit cards: all major
Restaurant
Nearest airport: Badajoz (61 km)
Nearest train station: Mérida

The Vía de la Plata (named after a Roman road) is installed in a historic church cum convent cum hospital cum jail dating back to the 15th century. There is, in addition, strong archaeological evidence pointing to the conclusion that this was originally the site of the Concordia Temple of Augustus during the Roman occupation of Mérida. There are ancient artifacts scattered throughout the large, whitewashed hotel - all discovered nearby. The architecture is a crazy mix: for example, in the gorgeous, Andalusian interior patio you will discover elegant mudejar-style pillars with Roman and Visigoth stones, and the stunning front sitting room was the convent chapel. The Vía de la Plata was recently renovated, to include an overall facelift, additional rooms and underground parking. The whitewashed rooms are very pleasant, with dark Spanish furniture, and many have domed ceilings and colorful rugs brightening the red-tile floors. The doubles in back have balconies and overlook the delightful Moorish gardens. All in all this is a charming, unusual parador.

P.N. VIA DE LA PLATA
Plaza de la Constitución, 3
06850 Mérida, Badajoz
tel: (24)313800
82 rooms - Pts 9,500
Credit cards: all major
Restaurant, ancient convent
U.S. Rep: NIC Tours
Rep tel: (415) 871-6680
Nearest airport: Badajoz (61 km)
Nearest train station: Mérida

Tucked in the peaceful hills slightly inland from Marbella is a hotel we prefer to the modern resorts on the coast. Ascend the mountain into this charming little white town and the enchanting sparkling white, Andalusian-style complex of the Hotel Mijas. The lobby, a stunning mixture of beautiful antiques and elegant regional furniture, features the backdrop of expansive views of Fuengirola and the Mediterranean. Although not small, the hotel is very personal and intimate. Your room will please you as much as the warmth of management, especially if you pay the slightly higher price for one with a view of the sea. Enhancing the view is the tasteful, muted, Andalusian decor of the rooms and the bottle of cold champagne that awaits your arrival. If just sitting on the terrace and gazing at the sea beyond the green hills is not active enough for you, there are two outdoor pools, an exercise area with an indoor pool and sauna, and tennis courts at the hotel, and golf and horseback riding nearby.

HOTEL MIJAS
Tamisa
29650 Míjas, Málaga
tel: (52)485800 telex: 77393
100 rooms - Pts 13,900
Credit cards: all major
Restaurant, pool, tennis
U.S. Rep: Best Western
Rep tel: 800-528-1234
Nearest airport: Málaga (32 km)
Nearest train station: Málaga (32 km)

Perched at the edge of a one-hundred-foot cliff overlooking the blue Mediterranean, this is a modern parador.   Featuring just a few antique touches in the halls
and public rooms, it still offers an attractive alternative to the posh and expensive
Costa del Sol resorts.   This parador is an excellent choice for those who want to
wind up their trip with a few days at the beach.   The extremely spacious public
areas are Spanish contemporary in decor, and make extensive use of glass to
capitalize on the marvelous view.   The Andalusian-style central patio is quite
pretty, with plants and flowers and a typical little fountain.   The result is a colorful
and relaxed atmosphere.   In the back, overlooking the sea, is a large park-like area
for lounging around the large pool.   At the corner of the park, twenty-five cents
buys an elevator ride down to a beautiful, giant sandy beach, with ample bars and
restaurants, and rental facilities.   After a day in the sun, you can return to an air-
conditioned, spacious room that commands the same view as the public rooms.

P.N. DE NERJA
Avda. Rodríguez Acosta, s/n
29780 Nerja, Málaga
tel: (52)520050
fax: 521997
73 rooms - Pts 11,000
Credit cards: all major
Restaurant, tennis, pool
U.S. Rep: NIC Tours
Rep tel: (415) 871-6680
Nearest airport: Málaga (52 km)
Nearest train station: Málaga (52 km)

This hotel was originally a monastery, established by Cistercian monks in 1194, and active until 1835, when it was abandoned and tragically ransacked. For services rendered during the Carlist war of succession - and a nominal fee - General Prim came into this particular piece of property, and his descendants own it to this day. Curiously, because of the monastery's uninhabited period, neighboring villages can claim parts of it, too, as evidenced by some fabulous works of art (such as choirstalls, altars, furniture - even wine vats) that grace their otherwise relatively humble holy places. The site is large and rich in history, having fine architectural examples from the Gothic through the Baroque periods. Wander at will, exploring every exciting corner, then enter the hotel from the beautiful cloisters. The antique-lined marble hallways must be twenty feet wide and thirty feet high, with arched ceilings, through which it seems the slightest sound echoes endlessly, and the incredible windows that appear to be covered with parchment are actually made of alabaster. The wood-floored bedrooms are, not surprisingly, the original monks' cells, and therefore simply but nicely furnished, and overlook a natural park, an interior patio or the cloister. Your stay here is guaranteed to be unforgettable.

HOTEL MONASTERIO DE PIEDRA
50210 Nuévalos, Zaragoza
tel: (76)849011
61 rooms - Pts 5,700
Credit cards: all major
Restaurant, tennis, pool
Nearest airport: Zaragoza (118 km)
Nearest train station: Alhama de Aragón (20 km)

This hotel used to be part of the parador chain, but was recently ceded to the regional government of Andalusia. Its somewhat isolated location provides a delightful contrast to the cosmopolitan coastal area and is obviously a destination for travelers with a car. Everything here says relax and settle in for a few days. In keeping with its hunting-lodge origin, the decor is comfortably rustic with the emphasis on heavy wood furnishings. There are several cozy lounges, one especially attractive with a fireplace and numerous trophies. The restaurant is extremely inviting and specializes in excellent game dishes, which makes it popular with locals in Marbella, especially in the evening. The rooms are simple and attractive and offer every comfort, including large modern bathrooms. If you plan to be here between late fall and early spring, you might request room number 3, since it has its own little fireplace. But the stellar attraction of this hotel is its natural setting - a pine forest loaded with peace and quiet and, in the summer, a cool, shady terrace where you can breakfast to the scent of pine. There is also a small pool, made all the more pleasant by its surrounding towering pine trees.

REFUGIO DE JUANAR
Sierra Blanca, s/n
29600 Ojén, Málaga
tel: (52)881000
23 rooms - Pts 5,650
Credit cards: all major
Restaurant, pool, tennis
Nearest airport: Málaga (65 km)
Nearest train station: Cartama (38 km)

Olite was the medieval capital of the Kingdom of Navarre, and Charles III made this castle fortress his summer residence in the early 15th century. Part of the extensive original dwelling has been incorporated into a charming parador (named after the young prince who spent his childhood here) which offers the modern-day resident unique lodging in this ancient walled town. Situated next to a tiny, elaborate church on a tranquil tree-lined plaza, the inn has an impressive, almost intimidating stone facade but, once inside, you will be delighted with the warm red-tile floors, stained glass, antiques, suits of armor and intimate bar and dining room. Only sixteen of its bedrooms are in the historic building, and they are wonderful, with canopied beds and wood floors; some still sheltered by crude exterior walls dating back hundreds of years, and two (rooms 36 and 37) with massive stone fireplaces. The "new" rooms are also lovely (and larger), decorated in subtle earth colors, with traditional Spanish wood furniture and floors. But if you prefer to stay in the old part, be sure you request "la parte vieja" when making your reservation.

P.N. PRINCIPE DE VIANA
Plaza de los Teobaldos, 2
31390 Olite, Navarra
tel: (48)740000
43 rooms - Pts 9,000
Credit cards: all major
Restaurant
U.S. Rep: NIC Tours
Rep tel: (415) 871-6680
Nearest airport: Pamplona (43 km)
Nearest train station: Olite

In the 14th century King Henry granted the medieval town of Oropesa, with its ancient castle, to don García Alvarez de Toledo, who gradually restored the castle and added to it, as did his descendants. Converted to a parador in 1930, the recently remodeled hotel has handsome bedrooms with thick beige rugs on red and blue tiled floors, beige bedspreads, rich wood furniture, ceramic and iron fixtures, and cavernous dazzling-white bathrooms. All but a few overlook the fertile Sierra de Gredos valley; the others look over the interior patio (originally a bullring), a 15th century Jesuit church and the remains of the ancient castle. This parador is home to an international cooking school, and the cuisine exceeds usual parador standards, as does the dining room itself, laid out on two levels, with skylights, painted-wood ceiling and large picture windows. In the lounge areas cozy leather furniture and exquisite antiques cluster around big stone fireplaces. In the basement is a tiny cell where Saint Peter of Alcántara chose to stay when he visited here - it is intriguing, but he might have chosen differently could he have seen the accommodations available now.

P.N. VIRREY TOLEDO
Plaza del Palacio, 1
45560 Oropesa, Toledo
tel: (25)430000
fax: 430777
44 rooms - Pts 8,000
Credit cards: all major
Restaurant, medieval castle
U.S. Rep: NIC Tours
Rep tel: (415) 871-6680
Nearest airport: Madrid (169 km)
Nearest train station: Oropesa

This hospitable hideaway is located at the junction of C430 and C431 on the Guadalquivir river, midway between Sevilla and Córdoba. A Franciscan monastery from the 16th to the 19th centuries, it once sheltered and educated monks on their way to missions in the New World, including the recently canonized Fray Junípero Serra, famous evangelizer of California. In 1828, when church property was being confiscated by the state all over Spain, the monastery passed into private hands - and subsequent ruin. It was eventually inherited by the Moreno family who, with care and attention to original historical detail, restored it over a three-year period, opening the tiny hotel to the public in 1987. (The family also raises fighting bulls, and the manager will happily arrange a visit to their ranch, if you're interested.) Tucked behind whitewashed walls in the heart of the typical Andalusian town of Palma del Río, you'll discover a superlative restaurant and cozy bar with artesonado ceilings, gardens and orchards, and a beautiful cloistered patio supporting a gallery around which the guestrooms are situated. The twin-bedded, air-conditioned rooms are simple and comfortable, decorated in earth tones with dark-wood furniture and trim. They have modern, colorfully tiled baths and small sitting areas. Rooms 5-8 are particularly spacious and original. The addition of eight rooms and a pool are in the works for the near future. The Hospedería offers unique and economical accommodation not far off the beaten track.

HOSPEDERIA DE SAN FRANCISCO
Avenida Pío XII, s/n
14700 Palma del Río, Córdoba
tel: (57)644185
8 rooms - Pts 6,000
Credit cards: all major
Superior restaurant
Nearest airport: Sevilla (82 km)
Nearest train station: Palma del Río

Situated in the shadow of the ancient fortified town of Puebla de Sanabria - crowned with a picture-perfect plaza and 15th century castle - is the whitewashed, 20th century parador of the same name. This roadside inn is not "historic" but, constructed in 1945, it dates back to the time when the government chain had less than 10 hotels and each one had just four double and four single rooms. It has since been remodeled and enlarged five times, and although it is quite unremarkable from without, it is pleasant and comfortable within. The marble floors in the lobby and lounges positively gleam due to constant polishing. Leather sling chairs and low tables lend a rustic, traditional Spanish flavor to the intimate, wood-paneled bar. There are stone fireplaces in the two cozy reading rooms and the dining room has picture windows and a nice wood ceiling. The bedrooms vary in size, but they are all whitewashed and spotless, rescued from austerity by the lovely dark Castilian furnishings, parquet floors and soft-colored drapes and spreads. The countryside views from the rooms are appealing and tranquil. Explore from here the enchanting village across the river and the marvelous lake area to the north.

P.N. PUEBLA DE SANABRIA
49300 Puebla de Sanabria, Zamora
tel: (88)620001
44 rooms - Pts 7,500
Credit cards: all major
Restaurant
U.S. Rep: NIC Tours
Rep tel: (415) 871-6680
Nearest airport: Valladolid (184 km)
Nearest train station: Puebla de Sanabria

Tucked in the shadows of the snowcapped Guadarrama mountain range, surrounded by pine forest, and within hailing distance of the ski area of Navacerrada, is the serene retreat of Santa María de El Paular. Less than two hours from Madrid, and located just outside the attractive village of Rascafría, the hotel is ensconced in the former living quarters of a monastery dating from the 14th century (and abandoned in the 19th) - in fact, the attached monastery is still active. Currently part of the well-known Italian CIGA hotel chain, it has been carefully restored and remodeled, and the most has been made of its marvelous original stone patios, columns and stairways. Don't miss the small, barren chapel just left of the arch leading to the entry patio (complete with fountain, and outdoor tables in warm weather). In it you'll discover a striking figure of the black virgin Nuestra Señora de Montserrat. Inside the hotel, you'll appreciate the handsome public rooms with beamed ceilings supporting iron chandeliers, wood and red-tile floors and capacious and cozy Castilian-style furnishings. The guestrooms - all offering tranquil vistas - are roomy, simple and handsome, with provincial wood furniture, hardwood floors and woven, earthtone bedspreads and drapes. And, to top it all off, the dining room provides above-average cuisine, and the management arranges horseback excursions.

HOTEL STA. MARIA DE EL PAULAR
28741 Rascafría, Madrid
tel: (1)8691011 telex: 23222
58 rooms - Pts 13,000
Credit cards: all major
Superior restaurant and lovely pool area
Nearest airport: Madrid (95 km)
Nearest train station: Navacerrada (11 km)

Around the turn of the century, British residents of "the rock" of Gibraltar used to come to Ronda for its cooler climate. In 1906, a hotel was built to house these British visitors and it was called the Queen Victoria. Although its interior has been remodeled and it is now a member of the extensive HUSA Spanish hotel chain, from the outside it betrays its non-Spanish origins. The public rooms are a mix of Victorian and modern decor. Some of the small sitting rooms are dominated by giant gilt-framed mirrors and boast Victorian furnishings, while the bar-cafeteria is decorated in rather ordinary contemporary Spanish style. The bedrooms are large and attractively fitted out with matching Victorian-style furniture. About forty of them have views of the famous Ronda Gorge from their terraces, while the others look out on the pretty grounds whose paths lead down to the very edge of the gorge and whose gardens are shaded by giant trees. A large pool with its own tree-covered island and a smaller pool for children are surrounded by an expansive lounge area with a terrace overlooking the same spectacular view.

HOTEL REINA VICTORIA
Jerez, 25
29400 Ronda, Málaga
tel: (52)871240
88 rooms - Pts 8,900
Credit cards: all major
Restaurant, pool
U.S. Rep: NIC Tours
Rep tel: (415) 871-6680
Nearest airport: Málaga (120 km)
Nearest train station: Ronda

In 1932 this luxurious "hostal" opened in the tiny fishing village of S'Agaro with just six rooms. The Gavina (seagull) and the resort town have come a long way since then, but the inn has remained in the Ensesa family, which is personally responsible for the extraordinary collection of antiques found throughout the premises. Everything you see - rugs, tapestries, tile, furnishings - is genuine; not a single reproduction blemishes the scene. Nor does a single room reproduce another; each is unique, and all are wonderful, spacious and bright. Careful attention has been given to the tiniest detail in every corner of every room (a man is employed full-time to do nothing but polish the wood). This is a hotel of a style and quality of a bygone era, as we are certain such previous guests as Frank Sinatra, Sylvester Stallone and Orson Welles would agree. The hotel is surrounded by lovely gardens, and has a divine pool overlooking the ocean which features fine poolside dining. You are a mere five-minute walk from the beach which draws a jet-set crowd in the summer. Do not fail to reserve well in advance during the high season.

HOSTAL DE LA GAVINA
17248 S'Agáro, Gerona
tel: (72)32-11-00 telex: 57132
fax: 321573
75 rooms - Pts 27,500
Open: March 22 to October 21
Credit cards: all major
Restaurant, pool, tennis
U.S. Rep: NIC Tours
Rep tel: (415) 871-6680
Nearest airport: Barcelona (103 km)
Nearest train station: Gerona (38 km)

The Gran Hotel is around the corner from the most exquisite central square in Spain - the arcaded Plaza Mayor - lined on all sides with close to one hundred perfectly symmetrical arches, and featuring thirteen outdoor cafes, to which tourists and natives alike flock in warm weather. Having recently passed its 50th birthday, the Gran Hotel is a little worn around the edges, but evidence of its former grandeur is still apparent. The austere, square stone façade belies the ornateness of the spacious lounges and the quiet elegance of the outstanding Feudal restaurant. A handsome stairway leads to the upper floors, where high-ceilinged, pleasant, but otherwise unremarkable bedrooms provide modern comfort and contemporary decor. Due to its location, the streets around the hotel are heavily trafficked, so you may want to sacrifice an exterior view for the peace and quiet of an inside room. It would be wise to take advantage of the inexpensive hotel garage. From the Gran Hotel you are within 15-minutes' walking distance of everything there is to see in this medieval, golden city, so rich in history that it has been proclaimed a national monument.

GRAN HOTEL
Y RESTAURANTE FEUDAL
Plaza Poeta Iglesias, 5
37001 Salamanca
tel: (23)213500 telex: 26809
100 rooms - Pts 11,000
Credit cards: all major
Restaurant
Nearest airport: Madrid (206 km)
Nearest train station: Salamanca

This ultra-modern parador overlooks the captivating city of Salamanca from across the Tormes river, spanned by an ancient Roman footbridge. In startling contrast to the majority of the Spanish government's "inns", this angular, glass-and-concrete structure is of no historical interest, although exceeding the normal parador standards of comfort. The lobby is a vast expanse of gleaming grey marble, softened by traditional wood and leather furniture on woven cream-colored rugs. Off to one side is a bar, and to the other a spacious lounge - both cozy and comfortable despite their size and contemporary setting. Best of all, along the length of the city-side wall is an uninterrupted picture window, with an outdoor terrace beyond, whose vista, especially at night, will take your breath away. Each floor has its own glass-enclosed terrace, with the same view, which you also enjoy from the bedrooms. The bedrooms are tastefully contemporary, decorated in subtle colors, with wood floors and extra-large baths. This lovely parador proves that the chain is not limited to successful reconstruction but, with some imagination and good taste, can also construct a pleasing modern hotel.

P.N. DE SALAMANCA
Teso de la Feria, 2
37007 Salamanca
tel: (23)268700
108 rooms - Pts 9,000
Credit cards: all major
Restaurant, pool
U.S. Rep: NIC Tours
Rep tel: (415) 871-6680
Nearest airport: Madrid (206 km)
Nearest train station: Salamanca

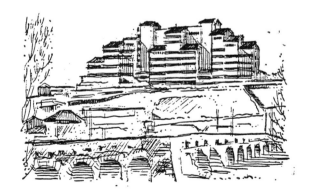

The Reyes Católicos is one of the most magnificent inns in Spain, recently acquired by the parador chain.   In the 15th century the building housed a pilgrims' hospice, which nurtured the sick and sheltered the humble who journeyed from all parts of Europe to visit the tomb of St. James.   The "hostal" has four interior patios (Matthew, Mark, Luke and John) overlooked by enclosed third-floor gallery-lounge areas lined with antiques.   The fabulous central court (where a music festival is held every August) has a fifty-foot ceiling and beautiful stained-glass windows. Each room, hallway, ceiling and floor is something special.   In addition to its rich history, the Reyes Católicos offers truly sumptuous accommodation for the modern pilgrim.   No two rooms are exactly alike, and the attention to detail is unsurpassed, resulting in harmonious old-world decor. The green-marble bathrooms are immense, featuring separate bath and shower and heated towel racks.   In a city that must be visited, this is a hotel than cannot be missed, even if you merely take a tour (it is the second most popular tourist attraction in Santiago after the cathedral.)

HOSTAL DE LOS REYES CATOLICOS
Plaza de España, 1
15705 Santiago de Compostela, La Coruña
tel: (81)582200 telex: 86004
158 rooms - Pts 16,000
Credit cards: all major
Restaurant, 16th century building
U.S. Rep: NIC Tours
Rep tel: (415) 871-6680
Nearest airport: Santiago
Nearest train station: Santiago

The Gil Blas - named after the infamous character in Le Sage's 18th century picaresque novel - sits on the cobblestoned main square in the heart of the tiny medieval village of Santillana.   Originally, the 15th century manor house, with its imposing stone façade and iron balconies, was the ancestral home of an important local family.   Now it provides the modern-day guest a temporary home while visiting this enchanting town and the area's fascinating archaeological discoveries. The entryway opens into a spacious, cobblestoned inner patio with massive stone walls and heavy antiques.   There is also a pretty interior garden where supper is served in warm weather.   The hallways and charming sitting areas on each floor are planked with dark wood, imbuing the hotel with a rich old-world flavor.   The bedrooms are whitewashed and wood-beamed, and furnished with many period pieces.   Only some have terraces, but all have nice views - the choices being onto the bustling central plaza, narrow side streets or the tranquil inside garden.   The Gil Blas and Santillana define the term quaint.

P.N. GIL BLAS
Plaza Ramón Pelayo, 11
39330 Santillana del Mar, Cantabria
tel: (42)818000
56 rooms - Pts 11,000
Credit cards: all major
Restaurant
U.S. Rep: NIC Tours
Rep tel: (415) 871-6680
Nearest airport: Santander (30 km)
Nearest train station: Torrelavega (15 km)

Flanked by pretty gardens, the handsome stone façade of the Hotel Los Infantes blends beautifully with the medieval village of Santillana.   The 18th century façade of this typical mountain manor was moved stone by stone from the nearby town of Orena and faithfully reconstructed here.   Over the doorway are two carved escutcheons - one bearing King Felipe V's coat of arms; the other that of Calderon, the original landlord.   The reception area and the first-floor salon are filled with antiques and are perfectly charming, with wood floors and beamed ceilings.   The breakfast room on the main floor, with its central fireplace, and the good dining room downstairs are not original, but are cozy and filled with old-world decor. Unfortunately, the bedrooms, with few exceptions, are smallish and rather plain, though consistently spotless and equipped with modern bathrooms and tiny terraces overlooking the gardens.   The three front-facing doubles with sitting rooms, wooden balconies and antique touches cost a little more but are the best rooms in the house.   Los Infantes offers reasonable accommodation with historical flavor.

HOTEL LOS INFANTES
Avenida Le Dorat, 1
39330 Santillana del Mar, Cantabria
tel: (42)818100
30 rooms - Pts 6,900
Credit cards: VS MC
Cafeteria
Nearest airport: Santander (30 km)
Nearest train station: Torrelavega (15 km)

In the 12th century, Saint Dominic built a shelter and hospital on the site of an old palace belonging to the Kings of Navarre.   His goal was humanitarian: a wayside hospice for pilgrims who passed through here on their arduous journey to Santiago. Today it houses a recently remodeled parador that offers unique accommodation in the quaint old town in the heart of Rioja wine country.   The town of Haro, home to numerous fine bodegas, is only 10 miles away.   The entrance of the hotel is through a small lobby into a vast lounge, buttressed by massive stone pillars and arches, with a wood-beamed ceiling and stained-glass skylight.   The dining room is unusual, too, with dark, rough-hewn wood pillars throughout, and the tables interspersed between them.   The bedrooms are plain by parador standards, though they live up to them in size and comfort, with traditional Spanish wooden furniture and floors.   Those in the old part are similar to those in the new.   However, the first-floor, front-facing doubles also have small terraces overlooking the quiet plaza, across to the cathedral and a church.

P.N. DE SANTO DOMINGO
Plaza del Santo, 3
26250 Santo Domingo de la Calzada,
La Rioja
tel: (41)340300
27 rooms - Pts 8,500
Credit cards: all major
Restaurant
U.S. Rep: NIC Tours
Rep tel: (415) 871-6680
Nearest airport: Vitoria (63 km)
Nearest train station: Haro (16 km)

The Linajes is (not easily) found down one of the tiny stone streets that crisscross Segovia's quaint old quarter, the barrio of San Esteban, which sits on a hill above the modern city.   Known as "The House of the Lineages", the warm-stone and aged-wood façade of the hotel is beautifully preserved from the 11th-century palace of the noble Falconi family, whose escutcheon can still be seen over the arched entryway.   Inside, with the exception of the pleasantly modern bar/cafeteria downstairs, the hotel conserves a charming old-Castile flavor, with dark wood, beamed ceilings and burnished-tile floors.   A cozy alcove off the lobby, decorated with wonderful antiques, looks into a glass-enclosed garden patio on one side, and over the open terrace in back, sharing its panoramic views over the city's monumental skyline.   There are lovely views from every bedroom, too.   The rooms in the newer part are carpeted and comfortable, accented in golds and browns, with contemporary Spanish furnishings.   However, those in the old part, though similarly furnished and decorated, remain favorites, with their wooden floors and views of the countryside through the original windows.

HOTEL LOS LINAJES
Dr. Velasco, 9
40003 Segovia
tel: (11)431201
55 rooms - Pts 7,750
Credit cards: all major
Restaurant, garage
Nearest airport: Madrid (89 km)
Nearest train station: Segovia

Segovia's parador is one of the few ultramodern offerings within the government-run chain, but, in accordance with its consistently high standards, it is a cut above any other contemporary competitor in service and style.   Situated on a hill outside Segovia, the parador commands spectacular panoramas of the golden, fortified city. The hotel's architecture is every bit as dramatic as its setting: huge brick and concrete slabs jut up and out at intriguing angles, topped by tile roofs and surrounded by greenery.   The angled brick-and-concrete motif is carried inside, where black-marble floors glisten beneath skylights in the enormous lobby. Picture windows frame Segovia beyond a garden terrace with a pretty pool.   The decor throughout is tasteful, Spanish contemporary; the feeling open, airy and bright.   The bedrooms are spacious and decorated in earth tones, with pale wood furniture.   Each has a balcony which shares the incomparable city view.   The combination of the modern and the historical has an unforgettable impact on the guest here, that being the hallmark of Spain's paradors.

P.N. DE SEGOVIA
Carretera N601
40003 Segovia
tel: (11)430462
80 rooms - Pts 10,000
Credit cards: all major
Restaurant, indoor/outdoor pool
U.S. Rep: NIC Tours
Rep tel: (415) 871-6680
Nearest airport: Madrid (89 km)
Nearest train station: Segovia

Constructed on the 14th-century site of the church and convent of Santo Domingo, and next door to a 12th-century cathedral, this is nonetheless a parador whose byword is modern. But, as with all hotels in this government chain, the accommodations are something special. Of the original building, only the old cloister has been preserved, and converted into one of the most spectacular lounges we have come across. Graceful stone arches form the foundation of a square central room, several stories high, bedecked with hanging plants and decorated with soft contemporary furnishings. And the dining room, with its glass ceiling and wicker and chrome furniture, is sunny, bright and attractive, as is the indoor pool - a rarity in Spain. In interesting contrast to most other paradors, and certainly to its setting, the bedrooms are strikingly modern in decor, spacious with wine-red furnishings, pale woven bedspreads and black rubber floors. The demisuites, 121 and 221, are a few dollars more but offer enormous space for the price. Situated in a fertile valley, Seo de Urgel is surrounded by the sierras of Arcabell and Cadi.

P.N. DE LA SEO DE URGEL
Santo Domingo
25700 Seo de Urgel, Lérida
tel: (73)352000
84 rooms - Pts 6,500
Credit cards: all major
Restaurant, pool
U.S. Rep: NIC Tours
Rep tel: (415) 871-6680
Nearest airport: Barcelona (200 km)
Nearest train station: Puigcerda (51 km)

When the need for a fine hotel in Seville - one of the most popular tourist destinations in Spain - became apparent, architect Espinau y Muñoz rose beautifully to the task, creating the Alfonso XIII in an Andalusian style unique to that city and calling upon local artisans for its decor.   Dedicated by its namesake, the Alfonso XIII is reminiscent of an opulent Moorish palace, surrounded by gardens, with fabulous artesonado ceilings, marble pillars, graceful mudéjar arches and colorful hand-painted ceramic tiles throughout.   The interior patio with its tinkling central fountain is elegant and peaceful, offering the perfect setting for relaxing with a cool drink at the end of a hot day.   All of the public rooms are stunning: wide marble staircases lead to expansive landings on each floor, decorated with fine antiques under elaborate carved ceilings.   Although some are more spacious than others, the high-ceilinged bedrooms are richly decorated in soft colors and handsome, classic wood furnishings.   Many have Spanish "oriental" rugs, specially made to fit.   Some second floor rooms have terraces over the patio.

HOTEL ALFONSO XIII
San Fernando, 2
41004 Seville
tel: (54)222850 telex: 72725
fax: 216033
149 rooms - Pts 26,000
(July and August: 15,100)
Credit cards: all major
Restaurant, gardens, pool
U.S. Rep: NIC Tours
Rep tel: (415) 871-6680
Nearest airport: Seville
Nearest train station: Seville

The Dóna María is a special hotel, located in the heart of Seville across from the famous Giralda; in fact it features a rooftop pool (beside which a duet plays on summer evenings) at eye level with the magnificent spire.   This was originally the palace of Peter the Cruel's administrator, and its present owner is the Marquesa de San Joaquín, who still resides there in her private suites, and who is personally responsible for the decoration of each and every room.   Each bedroom is dedicated to an illustrious Sevillian woman.   The lobby of the hotel is charming, with a domed ceiling and brick pillars, an intimate wood-paneled bar and lots of old-world atmosphere.   Its tiny interior garden is glass-enclosed and flanked by suits of armor.   The Doña María has added rooms over the years, so not all are in the original building.   The real charmers are each unique and in the "parte antigua".   A sampling: number 305 on the interior patio has beautiful twisted-wood canopy beds; number 310 is all white, with a double, brass-canopy bed and a smashing view of the Giralda, and number 103 has a fabulous double brass bed, decorated in deep red and cream.   Excellent location and ambiance for the price.

HOTEL DOÑA MARIA
Don Remundo, 19
41004 Seville
tel: (54)224990
61 rooms - Pts 11,000
Credit cards: AX VS DC
No restaurant, pool
Nearest airport: Seville
Nearest train station: Seville

Named for the king who led the reconquest of Seville and who is buried in her cathedral, this whitewashed hotel is surrounded by the picturesque alleyways of the historic Alfalfa quarter, and located just minutes by foot from all of the prominent sights in Andalusia's capital.   Though old-world ambiance does not characterize the Fernando III, contemporary comfort and attentive service at a reasonable price do.   The expansive, marble-floored and wood-beamed lobby fairly gleams, setting the tone for the guestrooms which, although not luxurious, are spacious and spotless, with high ceilings and roomy, modern baths.   Their predominantly green decor is consistent throughout, the only variation being whether a room has twins or a double bed, and is with or without a terrace.   In the case of the Fernando III, especially during warm weather, the additional 1,000 pesetas for a terrace affords a genuine enhancement, since the tiled balcony/patios are large and lovely and overlook the barrio's twisting, narrow streets.   Other attractive features include a parking garage (a real benefit in downtown Seville), a pool and air conditioning, both of which make a summer sojourn more enjoyable.

HOTEL FERNANDO III
San José, 21
41004 Seville
tel: (54)217307 telex: 72491
156 rooms - Pts 7,980
Credit cards: AX VS DC
Restaurant, pool, garage
Nearest airport: Seville
Nearest train station: Seville

Seville is famous for its enchanting Santa Cruz Quarter (barrio), and the Murillo is situated within it.   Only pedestrians can navigate the maze of streets in the barrio, so it is necessary to park outside the quarter - but a porter with a handcart will accompany you back to your car for your luggage.   Built in "barrio" style by the owner, Don Miguel, the whitewashed hotel faces a narrow stone street overhung by iron lanterns and balconies, a setting which offers incomparable tranquility in this bustling city.   Prior to his reincarnation as a hotelier over 20 years ago, Don Miguel was an antique dealer and wood craftsman, both apparent from the moment you arrive.   The doors and ceiling are hand-carved, and the lobby is chock-full of antiques, including suits of armor.   However, the Murillo's charm is almost spent in the lobby.   The hallways above are dotted with antiques, but the bedrooms are nothing fancy, just simple, clean accommodations with white marble-tiled floors and pseudo-traditional Spanish wood furniture.   Request an exterior room to take best advantage of the setting, and if one should fit your needs, there are a couple of small singles on the top floor that have terraces.

HOTEL MURILLO
Lope de Rueda, 7 y 9
41004 Seville
tel: (54)216095
61 rooms - Pts 7,500
Credit cards: all major
No restaurant
Nearest airport: Seville
Nearest train station: Seville

Next to the ramparts, in the ancient fortified town of Sos, birthplace of the Catholic King Ferdinand, is the new parador which bears his name. Despite its recent construction, the hotel blends harmoniously with the centuries-old buildings around it. The setting is enchanting - surrounded by the fertile campo real, resplendent with corn, wheat and hay. The serenity is interrupted only by the chirping of swallows and the clanking of cowbells. The hotel's location is convenient for exploring the narrow maze of streets lined with low, sunken doorways and stone escutcheons, and for venturing up to the Sada palace where Spain's most renowned king, and Machiavelli's model prince, was born. In the lobby is a statue of the *"reyito"* (little king) alongside his mother, Juana Enrique. Upstairs, the view can be enjoyed over coffee or cocktails on an outdoor terrace, and the dining room is cozy, with leather chairs, wood-beamed ceiling and elaborate iron chandeliers. The bedrooms have brick-red tile floors, colorful woven spreads and drapes, pretty brass and glass lamps, and simple iron and brass bedsteads. A few have terraces.

P.N. FERNANDO DE ARAGON
50680 Sos del Rey Católico, Zaragoza
tel: (48)888011
65 rooms - Pts 7,000
Closed: December 15 to January 15
Credit cards: all major
Restaurant
U.S. Rep: NIC Tours
Rep tel: (415) 871-6680
Nearest airport: Pamplona (59 km)
Nearest train station: Pamplona (59 km)

Less than a mile from the city of Teruel, incomparably graced with mudéjar architecture, is not surprisingly a recently remodeled parador. Surrounded by appealing grounds sheltering an attractive pool, the hotel has the appearance of a large private home, built in mudéjar style, with a warm yellow facade and gently sloping tiled roofs. The unusual, somewhat formal octagonal lobby, dotted with antiques, features marble pillars and a high sculpted ceiling. A massive stone archway frames marble stairs leading up to the bedrooms. The sunny glass-enclosed terrace off the dining room and bar has the feel of an atrium, with pretty pastel-colored, flowered upholstery and wicker furniture, making it an altogether inviting spot for cocktails or supper. The bedrooms are parador-large, with wood floors and woven earth-tone spreads on dark-wood beds. Although this is not a stellar example within the government chain, the hotel is nonetheless pleasant and commodious throughout, and it is unquestionably the best choice of accommodation when visiting the architecturally and archaeologically rich province and city of Teruel.

P.N. DE TERUEL
Carretera N 234
44000 Teruel
tel: (74)602553
60 rooms - Pts 8,500
Credit cards: all major
Restaurant
U.S. Rep: NIC Tours
Rep tel: (415) 871-6680
Nearest airport: Valencia (149 km)
Nearest train station: Teruel

This turn-of-the-century hotel appears as a grand old mansion - white with yellow awnings - surrounded by pine trees and a marvelous view of the inlet of Pontevedra. One of the finest white-sand beaches in Spain (La Lanzada) is five minutes away - a beautiful pool overlooks the inlet - and there are golf and a casino at hand for the more energetic. Famous among Europeans for decades for its thermal baths, this luxurious establishment is a true, world-class resort, preserving the best of the old style, while incorporating the best of modern convenience. The sparkling-white lobby offers the first taste of the elegant public rooms. The vast, grand dining room is stunning, with a huge stained-glass skylight and gleaming marble floors. There is an outside enclosed terrace for supping and dancing on summer evenings. The marvelous sun terrace looking out to the pool and the inlet (dotted with platforms for the cultivation of mussels) has a ceiling draped in yellow and white, a motif carried out in the upholstery on the white wicker furniture beside glass-topped tables. The bedrooms are spacious and modern, designed for the comfort of long-term guests. The Gran Hotel demands the time to be relished.

GRAN HOTEL
36991 Isla de la Toja, Pontevedra
tel: (86)730025 telex: 88042
201 rooms - Pts 17,300*
* * (includes breakfast)*
Credit cards: all major
Restaurant, pool, tennis, golf
Nearest airport: Vigo (62 km)
Nearest train station: Villagarcía (30 km)

Almazara translates as olive-oil press and identifies the purpose of this building before it was turned into a hotel in 1950. It once also served as a convent and, when built in 1560, it was the residence of Cardinal Mendoza, called the "Third King" because of his behind-the-scenes power during the reign of Ferdinand and Isabella. The owner has gone to great lengths to maintain the atmosphere - even to the point of constructing his own nearby residence in the same style. Like the parador, this modest hotel is outside of town on a hillside across the Tagus river, and thus requires a car, especially since the only meal served is breakfast. If you like a rural setting, however, and a good value, it is an excellent choice. The public areas are nicely appointed with regional decor and inviting with a cozy fireplace in the handsome lounge. The bedrooms are plain, but comfortably furnished, and seven of them have heart-stopping views of the city from large terraces. Be sure to request a terrace, for a nominal extra cost. The view of one of Spain's most beautiful cities is not quite as all-inclusive as the parador's since this hotel is farther from town, but the terrace at sunset is lovely, and a room here is less than half the price.

HOTEL LA ALMAZARA
Apartado Postal, 6
48080 Toledo
tel: (25) 223866
21 rooms - Pts 4,400
Open: March 15 to October 31
Credit cards: VS MC DC
Nearest airport: Madrid (80 km)
Nearest train station: Toledo

Originally only an exquisite restaurant, the hostal now also provides similarly wonderful lodgings in a former archbishop's summer home. The mansion is a real jewel, located only a stone's throw from the main city gate (Puerta de Bisagra). Enter from the parking lot through an 11th-century wall to find a marvelous garden with the outdoor restaurant on the left. Climb the stairs on the right to reach the tiny foyer of the hostal. This is the one negative about the place - it is something of a hike with luggage. Reflecting its 18th century heritage, the stunning stairway, the patio with its lovely fountain, and the cozy sitting rooms, embellished with antiques, are harmonious and tranquil. The indoor dining rooms (which are used only in the winter) are fabulous with their heavy wood beams and fireplaces. In warmer months dine outdoors in the shadow of the medieval walls on succulent Castilian specialties such as suckling pig. The period furnishings in the inviting guest rooms seem to blend into a tasteful whole. Although smallish, the rooms provide modern comfort with an unbeatable ambiance of past centuries all for a modest price, particularly when considering the quality and location.

HOSTAL DEL CARDENAL
Paseo Recaredo 24
45004 Toledo
tel: (25)224900
fax: 222991
27 rooms - Pts 6,900
Credit cards: all major
Excellent restaurant
Nearest airport: Madrid (80 km)
Nearest train station: Toledo

The ancient town of Toledo is probably the most beautiful in Spain, and this parador sits on the hillside across the Tagus river from it, and if ever you're willing to pay extra for a view and a terrace, this is the place to do so.   Of course, the bar and the restaurant both have terraces with a view, so you are paying for privacy - your own balcony and view.   We think it is worth every penny to see the city change from golden brown to pink in the setting sun.   In any case you will be happy with the rooms - large, comfortable and tastefully decorated with gaily colored wooden headboards and red-tile floors with pretty rugs.   The open-beamed ceilings are especially attractive.   Indeed, the whole regional-style building is handsome.   The impressive, two-story lobby with its giant wood beams is magnificent when viewed from the gallery above which leads to your room. Liberal use of colorful ceramic tiles and local copper pieces adds a delightful touch. There is also a pool surrounded by a pretty lawn.   As lovely as it is, however, its only drawback is that you have to drive into town.

P.N. CONDE DE ORGAZ
Paseo de los Cigarrales
45000 Toledo
tel: (25)221850 telex: 47998
fax: 225166
77 rooms - Pts 9,500
Credit cards - all major
Restaurant, pool
U.S. Rep: NIC Tours
Rep tel: (415) 871-6680
Nearest airport: Madrid (80 km)
Nearest train station: Toledo

Installed in the 16th century convent of Santa Clara, this newest addition to the parador chain, built in 1984, blends harmoniously with the Renaissance and medieval architecture in Trujillo.   Enter through the outdoor stone patio, and be sure to notice the *"torno"* (revolving shelf) to the right of the doorway.   The original residents were cloistered nuns, and it was by way of this device that they sold their homemade sweets to the town's citizens.   Inside, eighteen of the hotel's bedrooms were originally the nuns' cells, and retain their low, stone doorways. They surround a sunlit gallery overlooking a cloistered garden patio with an old stone well at its center.   Beyond that, new bedrooms surround another, whitewashed courtyard with a small turquoise swimming pool at its center. Although there is a special flavor to the original bedrooms, the new addition maintains a traditional Spanish look and feel with pale-wood furnishings, brick-tiled floors, leather sling chairs and iron fixtures.   This is a charming spot from which to launch explorations of Extremadura, whose native sons launched their own explorations to the New World.

P.N. DE TRUJILLO
Plaza de Santa Clara
10200 Trujillo, Cáceres
tel: (27)321350
fax: 321366
46 rooms - Pts 8,500
Credit cards: all major
Restaurant
U.S. Rep: NIC Tours
Rep tel: (212) 686-9213
Nearest airport: Madrid (252 km)
Nearest train station: Cáceres (42 km)

This parador sits on the banks of the calm blue Miño river, across from Portugal. In fact, if looking across the river from the right place on the terrace, you can see the Pousada de Sao Teotonio, Portugal's answer to a parador. The hotel's nice pool also overlooks the river. Tuy has two claims to fame, one being its proximity to the border-crossing bridge spanning the river; the other is the beautiful cathedral of Saint Bartholomew. The parador has also made its mark on this serene setting. Modeled after a traditional regional manor house, the relatively austere stone exterior (including crenellations) reflects the centuries-long struggle of the Galician culture against aggression from the south in Portugal, the east in Spain and the English pirates from the sea. Inside, the hotel is warm and inviting. The salon off the lobby has a rich wood ceiling and floor, and a wonderful corner fireplace supported by a stone pillar. A handsome, wide stairway leads upstairs to comfortable and spacious bedrooms, offering all the modern amenities while maintaining a traditional Spanish flavor. Though not the fanciest of paradors, this is an ideal spot for a day of rest and relaxation, sunshine and a swim.

P.N. SAN TELMO
36700 Tuy, Pontevedra
tel: (86)600309
22 rooms - Pts 8,500
Credit cards: all major
Restaurant, pool
U.S. Rep: NIC Tours
Rep tel: (415) 871-6680
Nearest airport: Vigo (28 km)
Nearest train station: Guillarei (2 km)

This parador is installed in a 16th-century palace on Ubeda's monumentally magnificent, Renaissance main square. It features no less than three interior patios, one lined by slender stone arches and dotted with outdoor tables, another overhung with its original wooden terraces and the third converted to a lovely garden. All but the five newest guestrooms are found at the glass-enclosed gallery level, up a massive stone stairway flanked by suits of armor. The hotel has undergone two renovations, resulting in a variety of rooms off the antique-lined hallways, all of them lovely, with gleaming white baths, colorfully tiled floors and wood artesonado ceilings. Our personal favorites are those overlooking the golden Plaza Vázquez de Molina and El Salvador chapel, largely furnished with antiques. A few bedrooms have terraces, but are slightly smaller, and the more recent additions are decorated in a modern style, and are more spacious (two with sitting rooms for an additional 1,800 pesetas). Detailed attention to faithful historical preservation is obvious throughout the parador's public rooms, with the exception of the recently constructed, but pleasant restaurant, whose menu offers an unusually creative variety of dishes. Don't miss a visit to the Taberna, a lounge/bar in the stone basement, whose decor includes huge, ceramic storage vats.

P.N. CONDESTABLE DAVALOS
Plaza de Vázquez Molina, s/n
23400 Ubeda, Jaén
tel: (53)750345
fax: 751259
31 rooms - Pts 10,000
Credit cards: all major
U.S. Rep: NIC Tours
Rep tel: (415) 871-6680
Nearest airport: Granada (120 km)
Nearest train station: Baeza/Linares (20 km)

Four kilometers west of the sleepy town of Verín, its brooding stone towers visible from afar, is the medieval castle fortress of Monterrey (the most important monument in the province of Orense), which faces the parador of the same name. Reached by driving through green vineyards, the hotel is constructed in the style of a regional manor, having a somewhat severe exterior of cut stone blocks with a crenellated tower at one end. This is most definitely a country inn, perched atop a vine-covered hill and surrounded by lovely views in all directions from its high vantage point. The lobby features warm wood decorated with suits of armor and other antique pieces. Fifteen of the 23 bedrooms enjoy the countryside vista, eight of which overlook the dramatic castle (ask for 102, 104, 106 or 107). The large rooms are pleasantly decorated in beige and brown, with wood floors and comfortable contemporary Spanish furniture. The tranquil setting of this parador, along with its pretty pool in the middle of a lovely green lawn and the delightfully cozy reading room with its unusual fireplace, makes it an ideal spot for overnighting, especially if you can squeeze in a visit to the castle and its 13th-century church.

P.N. MONTERREY
32600 Verín, Orense
Tel: (88)410075
23 rooms - Pts 7,500
Credit cards: all major
Restaurant, pool
U.S. Rep: NIC Tours
Rep tel: (415) 871-6680
Nearest airport: Vigo (180 km)
Nearest train station: La Godina (30 km)

Situated in the pine-green mountains outside the charming medieval town of Vich, this parador overlooks the broad blue Sau reservoir, fed under azure skies by the waters of the Ter river.   Its setting is singular in beauty and tranquility.   The hotel is within easy walking distance of an ancient monastery that can only be reached by foot and within easy driving distance of several of the most picturesque villages in the region, Rupit being the most notable example.   The building itself is styled after a typical Catalan farmhouse (*masia*), with a somewhat severe façade of pale-gray granite with arched windows, iron balconies and red-tile roof.   The two-story patio/lobby inside is graced by heavy polished-wood columns and has a vast stained-glass ceiling which casts blue and gold light on a shining white-marble floor. There is a gorgeous sitting room with antiques and a cozy fireplace.   The wood-paneled bar has a terrace with views over the lake below.   All of the bedrooms (with the exception of the suites) have terraces with splendid views over the lovely swimming pool and lawn and on to the hill-ringed lake beyond.   The rooms are large and pleasant, decorated with wooden furniture and lovely brass and iron lamps.

P.N. DE VICH
08500 Vich, Barcelona
tel: (3)8887211
fax: 8887311
36 rooms - Pts 9,000
Credit cards: all major
Restaurant, pool, tennis
U.S. Rep: NIC Tours
Rep tel: (415) 871-6680
Nearest airport: Barcelona (80 km)
Nearest train station: Vich (14 km)

This truly delightful small country inn is located just west of the sleepy village of Villalonga and only 3 kilometers from La Lanzada, one of the finest white-sand beaches in Spain.   The ivy-covered, 16th century, Galician manor house (pazo) is made of square-cut stone blocks, and is surrounded by verdant countryside and lovely gardens which shelter the hotel's pretty pool and tennis courts.   It looks just like all the other farmhouses in the area, but you are invited to stay here.   The arched stone entryway leads to a charming interior courtyard where meals are served "al aire libre" on the awning-covered patio off the dining room which features a wood-beamed ceiling and massive bare stone walls.   The lobby and lounge retain an old-world country flavor down to the last detail, with wood floors and ceilings and whitewashed walls.   The bedrooms are simply furnished, but appealingly decorated, with red-brick tile floors and warm wood furniture.   If you are looking for a "getaway" spot, with the feeling of being in the middle of nowhere, while still within walking distance of the ocean and easy driving distance of an exciting city - Santiago - this inn is hard to beat, but be sure to reserve well in advance.

HOTEL PAZO EL REVEL
Camino de la Iglesia
36990 Villalonga, Pontevedra
tel: (86)743000
22 rooms - Pts 7,600
Closed: September 1 to June 15
Pool, tennis
Nearest airport: Santiago (64 km)
Nearest train station: Pontevedra (25 km)

Cortés was the conquistador of the Aztec empire in Mexico in 1521. He was born in Medellín, east of Mérida, but was taken on as a protege by the Duke of Feria, whose ancestors built this wonderful fortified castle in the 15th century. Cortés actually lived here for a short time before embarking for Cuba as an ordinary colonist. The castle has been faithfully restored and put to use as a highly attractive hotel. Virtually surrounded by towers, the exterior is somewhat intimidating, but the tiny plaza in front of it is charming and, once inside, you will love the lounges and public areas with antiques in every available space. There is a glorious chapel with an incredible golden cupola, and the Sala Dorada, or golden room, has a beautiful ceiling. The central patio, with its graceful stone columns, is equally enchanting. The bedrooms vary somewhat, since they were often installed in the original castle rooms, but they are all attractively decorated with regional furniture and the traditional parador good taste. This parador affords a marvelous opportunity to lodge in an authentic castle without sacrificing a single modern comfort.

P.N. HERNAN CORTES
Plaza de María Cristina, s/n
06300 Zafra, Badajoz
tel: (24)550200
28 rooms - Pts 8,000
Credit cards: all major
Restaurant, pool
U.S. Rep: NIC Tours
Rep tel: (415) 871-6680
Nearest airport: Seville (135 km)
Nearest train station: Zafra

As is sometimes the case, this parador is rather austere from the outside - an old stone mansion built in the 15th century by the counts whose name it bears.   But its location is perfect for exploring the narrow, picturesque streets of the old quarter. Once you are inside, however, it will charm you as it did us.   The elaborate use of antiques with regional furniture makes a terrific impression.   The central patio, surrounded by glassed-in, stone-arcaded galleries, is wonderful.   Marvelous old tapestries and chivalric banners abound on the walls, and many of the interior doorways have intricately carved facades.   Sitting areas are arranged around the galleries and afford a lovely view through rich wood shutters of the interior patio with its old stone well.   The bedrooms are large and well-decorated in regional style.   Some rooms have a pretty view over the river and others over a small stone-paved plaza.   If you face the plaza, look for a family of nesting storks perched perilously atop the tower of the facing building.

P.N. CONDES DE ALBA Y ALISTE
Plaza de Viriato, 5
49001 Zamora
tel: (88)514497
27 rooms - Pts 9,000
Credit cards: all major
Restaurant, pool
U.S. Rep: NIC Tours
Rep tel: (415) 871-6680
Nearest airport: Valladolid (97 km)
Nearest train station: Zamora

INN DISCOVERIES FROM OUR READERS

Many hotel recommendations have been sent to us by you, our readers. Some we have included in this edition, others we have not yet had the opportunity to see. We have a rule never to include any hotel, no matter how perfect it sounds, until we have made a personal inspection. This seems a waste of some excellent "tips", so, to solve this dilemma, we are adding to each of our guides a new section of hotels you have seen and loved and have shared with us, but which we have not yet inspected. Thank you for your contributions.

BURGUETE	HOTEL LOIZU

Hotel Loizu, Unica, 51, 31640 Burguete, Navarra tel: (48)760008

Loizu is a quaint, inn in Burguete, a pretty little whitewashed, geranium-lined town at the foothills of the Pyrenees, halfway between Spanish Pamplona and French St Jean de Pied Port. Built around the turn of the century, this Tudor-beamed, mahogany-floored hostelry maintains its old charm and is still superbly run by the Loizu Family. Hemingway purportedly spent a few days here during his trout-fishing stint in the Irati River, hauntingly narrated in his "The Sun Also Rises". And with good reason: Loizu's hearty, home-cooked fare is famous among the gourmet Navarrese, attracting wedding receptions, parties and culinary "happenings". The inn has a varied clientele, ranging from Spanish summer vacationers to international guests during the October dove-hunting season, right athwart the busiest dove migration route in Europe. Thirty miles north of Pamplona, it makes for an ideal operating base during the frantic bull-running festival of San Fermin, in early July. For the history buff, Burguete sits at the crossroads of ancient events. A mile to the north, on the road to France, lies

Roncesvalles, a monastery which once ministered to weary pilgrims on the road to Santiago in northwestern Spain. Its 12th-century chapel is claimed to have been built on the very spot where Roland, Charlemagne's rearguard, commander of epic fame, met his untimely end. Three miles to the south lies Sorogain, the place of witches, with its haunting cromlech, where Basques performed their arcane rites in the mists of history. To top it all off, the price is right at the Loizu Inn; full room and board runs between $35 and $40 per person, per day. The hearty three-course meals served both at lunch and supper (including a bottle of Rioja-Navarra claret) would be a delight for famished wayfarers of yesteryear and today. Recommended by: Dr. J. M. Lacambra, Florida.

COSGAYA-POTES   HOTEL DEL OSO

Hotel del Oso, Carret. N621, 39539 Cosgaya, Cantabria, tel: (42)730418

Hidden up an Alpine valley in Cantabria is a beautifully appointed discovery Hotel del Oso (translated to mean, "Hotel of the Bear") managed by Ana Rivas who was educated in England and has a wonderful command of the English language. Cosgaya-Potes is under 80 miles from Santander and close to the Parador "Rio Deva" in Fuente Dé. The hotel is a lovely stone home with an arched entry and wooden balcony that encircles the top floor. The home enjoys a gorgeous setting with the peaks of Europe at its back and a peaceful river that runs quietly at its side. It is an ideal spot for sport enthusiasts. A cable car at the end of the road will take you to the top of the beautiful mountains. One can trout fish in the small river that runs through the valley or, during season, one can deer hunt in the surrounding woods. The hotel also has one tennis court and a swimming pool (unheated). A double room runs around $40. Recommended by: Jim Moss, California.

FUENTERRABIA   HOTEL PAMPINOT

Hotel Pampinot, Nagusia 3, 20280 Fuenterrabía, Guipúzcoa, tel: (43) 640600

Located on the Calle Mayor, the Hotel Pampinot is just down the street from the P.N. El Emperador. It is a real gem with just eight rooms, all ultra luxurious in their furnishings and accommodation. The hotel is overflowing with handsome antiques and described as extremely fine. Although the hotel serves only breakfast, there is a delightful restaurant just two doors away - the Sebastián (Mayor, 7, tel: (43)640167). A double costs about $150. Recommended by: Jim Moss, California.

ALMUÑECAR   HOSTAL TROPICAL

Hostal Tropical, Europa 3, 18690 Almuñécar, tel: (58) 633458

As frequent travelers to the Costa Del Sol and avid readers of your books, we felt it was important to let you know of a very special place we found that has not fallen prey to the commercialism that has ruined most of the coast. The Hostal Tropical is only thirty feet from the beach and has clean new bathrooms in every room. The cost was only 2,500 pesetas a night for two people. Almuñécar is a lovely city to spend time walking in. Both beaches have the traditional esplanade along with thatch covered bars and restaurants. Almuñécar is about an hour's drive east of Malaga on the main road. Recommended by: Buzz and Laurie Remde, California.

Index

INN DISCOVERIES FROM OUR READERS

Future editions of *KAREN BROWN'S COUNTRY INN GUIDES* are going to include a new feature - a list of hotels recommended by our readers. We have received many letters describing wonderful inns you have discovered; however, we have never included them until we had the opportunity to make a personal inspection. This seemed a waste of some marvelous "tips". Therefore, in order to feature them we have decided to add a new section called "Inn Discoveries from Our Readers".

If you have a favorite discovery you would be willing to share with other travellers who love to travel the "inn way", please let us hear from you and include the following information:

1. *Your name, address and telephone number.*

2. *Name, address and telephone number of "your inn".*

3. *Brochure or picture of inn (we cannot return material).*

4. *Written permission to use an edited version of your description.*

5. *Would you want your name, city and state included in the book?*

We are constantly updating and revising all of our guide books. We would appreciate comments on any of your favorites. The types of inns we would love to hear about are those with special old-world ambiance, charm and atmosphere. We need a brochure or picture so that we can select those which most closely follow the mood of our guides. We look forward to hearing from you. Thank you.

Karen Brown's Country Inn Guides

The Most Reliable & Informative Series on Country Inns

Detailed itineraries guide you through the countryside and suggest a cozy inn for each night's stay. In the hotel section, every listing has been inspected and chosen for its romantic ambiance. Charming accommodations reflect every price range, from budget hideaways to deluxe palaces.

Order Form

KAREN BROWN'S COUNTRY INN GUIDES

Please ask in your local bookstore for KAREN BROWN'S COUNTRY INN guides. If the books you want are unavailable, you may order directly from the publisher.

AUSTRIAN COUNTRY INNS & CASTLES $12.95
CALIFORNIA COUNTRY INNS & ITINERARIES $12.95
ENGLISH, WELSH & SCOTTISH COUNTRY INNS $12.95
EUROPEAN COUNTRY CUISINE - ROMANTIC INNS & RECIPES $10.95
EUROPEAN COUNTRY INNS - BEST ON A BUDGET $14.95
FRENCH COUNTRY BED & BREAKFASTS $12.95
FRENCH COUNTRY INNS & CHATEAUX $12.95
GERMAN COUNTRY INNS & CASTLES $12.95
IRISH COUNTRY INNS $12.95
ITALIAN COUNTRY INNS & VILLAS $12.95
PORTUGUESE COUNTRY INNS & POUSADAS $12.95
SCANDINAVIAN COUNTRY INNS & MANORS $12.95
SPANISH COUNTRY INNS & PARADORS $12.95
SWISS COUNTRY INNS & CHALETS $12.95

Name _____   *Street* _____
City _____   *State* _____ *Zip* _____

Add $2.50 for the first book and .50 for each additional book for postage & packing.
California residents add 7% sales tax.
Indicate the number of copies of each title. Send in form with your check to:

KAREN BROWN'S COUNTRY INN GUIDES
P.O Box 70
San Mateo, CA 94401
(415) 342-9117

This guide is especially written for the individual traveller who wants to plan his own vacation. However, should you prefer to join a group, Town and Country - Hillsdale Travel can recommend tours using country inns with romantic ambiance for many of the nights' accommodation. Or, should you want to organize your own group (art class, gourmet society, bridge club, church group, etc.) and travel with friends, custom tours can be arranged using small hotels with special charm and appeal. For further information please call:

Town & Country - Hillsdale Travel
16 East Third Avenue
San Mateo, California 94401

(415) 342-5591

CYNTHIA and RALPH KITE admit to a long-term love affair with Spain, where they now live. Both are fluent in Spanish and intimately acquainted with the culture and customs of the Iberian Peninsula. Ralph is a professor of Hispanic Literature affiliated with a major American university and has authored several texts on the culture and language of the Spanish-speaking world. Cynthia has always had an interest in language and travel and has studied in Mexico, Spain and France. She holds a degree in Spanish and French, and is currently pursuing a writing career. Together, Cynthia and Ralph have visited almost every Latin country in the world and have traveled throughout Europe - west and east - as well as South America.

BARBARA TAPP, the talented professional artist who is responsible for most of the interior sketches in *Spanish Country Inns & Paradors*, always saves time from her busy art and homemaking schedule to help her friend Karen with the illustrations for her Country Inn guides. Born and raised in Sydney, Australia, Barbara now lives in the San Francisco Bay area with her husband, Richard, their two young sons, Jonathan and Alexander, and their baby daughter, Georgia.

CHRISTINA LADAS, who painted the cover for *Spanish Country Inns & Paradors*, was born and raised in the New York City area where she still resides with her little friend and helper, daughter Erena. The fact that Christina's mother, interior designer Zoe Ladas, recognized and encouraged her daughter's artistic abilities from a pre-school age contributes to her success today as a well-known artist whose wide range of talent leads her into almost every field of art.

Karen Brown (Herbert) was born in Denver, but has spent most of her life in the San Francisco Bay area where she now lives with her husband, Rick, their little girl, Alexandra, and baby son, Richard. Taking a year off from college, Karen travelled to Europe and wrote French Country Inns & Chateaux, the first in what has grown to be an extremely successful series of 14 guide books on charming places to stay. For many years Karen has been planning to open her own country inn. Her dream will soon come to reality - Karen and her husband, Rick, have bought a beautiful piece of property on the coast south of San Francisco and are working with an architect to design the "perfect" little inn which will be furnished with the antiques she has been collecting for many years and will incorporate her wealth of information on just what makes an inn very special. Karen and Rick are looking forward to welcoming guests and friends to their inn.